Major Contributors to Social Science Series

ALFRED MC CLUNG LEE, General Editor

Thorstein Veblen

BERNARD ROSENBERG

The City College of the City University of New York

THOMAS Y. CROWELL COMPANY

New York, Established 1834

Library of Congress Catalog Card Number: 63–9197
Series design by Laurel Wagner
Manufactured in the United States of America by The Colonial Press Inc.

Editor's Foreword

Undergraduates often find a great challenge in reading a seminal thinker's major contributions to social science in their original form. But students are usually offered either volume-length works containing stimulating passages embedded in outworn discussions, or brief excerpts included with those of other authors in general collections of readings. The longer works tend to be repetitious and wordy, and some now appear misguided. At the same time, excerpts in general collections do not give enough of a contributor's work to make him come alive.

In planning the present series, John T. Hawes, Director of the College Department of the Thomas Y. Crowell Company, and I sought manuscripts free from either of the above weaknesses. The editors were asked to dig out the main lines of a contributor's method and thought from the verbiage and the dated materials obscuring them, and to make available, in one slim volume, a critical essay together with the most significant and interesting passages in a contributor's writings. The volumes in the series, considered as a whole, thus give the student an understanding of the diverse ways of thought that have gone into the making of the social science discipline as we now know it.

The series has been edited and written so that each little book can be read for its own merits and without need of additional props. Each contains the seminal ideas of an author which still remain alive today but does not gloss over his weaknesses. Each book provides a critical vignette of the social scientist as he is now seen. Each book, too, should be interesting to college sophomores and especially to undergraduate majors in the various social sciences.

What all volumes in the series have in common is an educative conception. They are all efforts to interest undergraduates in some of the great "originals" of social science and thus to stimulate further exploration of important ideas and methods. The editor-critic who has done each volume has been free to follow his own professional judgment in analyzing his major contributor and in selecting significant excerpts from his works. Each volume thus has an individuality deriving from its editor-critic as well as from its subject.

The books in this series are intended to enrich introductory courses in the various social sciences. For more advanced courses, they will permit the student to become acquainted with the meatiest contributions of many selected social scientists rather than the few whose works he might read more extensively. Advanced students will find these books invaluable for the purposes of review.

ALFRED MC CLUNG LEE

Preface

Taken very seriously today, Thorstein Bunde Veblen was greatly neglected in his own day. *The Theory of the Leisure Class* and *The Theory of Business Enterprise* found few readers till after their author's death; some years later they had begun to assume the status of classics. By now Veblen's many neologisms are coin of the realm, and one or two of the ideas that went with them have been diffused to a sizable public.

This book is designed for those who do not yet know that there is much more to Veblen than a superficial scrutiny of his more popular work will yield. The full body of that work offers us an embarrassment of riches. One can do no more in a modest miscellany like this than to suggest the range and relevance of Veblen. He should appeal to the general reader with a taste for challenging thought—as he inevitably does to the student of philosophy, sociology, psychology, political science, anthropology, and economics. Exposure to the Veblenian canon (not necessarily its acceptance) can only be beneficial at a time of widespread obfuscation. Parts are hard going; all are rewarding provided they are read in the same critical spirit Veblen did so much to foster.

If the editor may be permitted a personal note, his Introduction is surely not the last word on Veblen, but it is *his* last word. Long ago (or so it seems) he allowed himself the indiscretion of a book called *The Values of Veblen*. The values still seem to him to be there, and he welcomes this opportunity to view them with as much maturity as he is ever likely to attain.

Thanks once more to Carl Mayer and Albert Salomon for the stimulus they have unfailingly provided, to Donna Whiteman for her help, to my wife, Sarah, and my children, Deena and Daniel, for their goodness.

B.R.

New York City, January, 1963

Contents

Thorstein Veblen

Introduction

No one remotely like Thorstein Veblen can ever be expected to appear again. As a man, as a scholar, and as a stylist, he was an original, always incomparably himself. This uniqueness makes it all the more ironic that Veblen should so often be put down as a derivative thinker. Talcott Parsons, the eminent but often indecipherable sociologist, has clearly stated, "Quite adequate comprehension of all Veblen's real contributions can be found in Weber's works." We shall have to inspect some of Veblen's "real contributions"; it will then become apparent that they cannot be found in Weber's works—which were probably more important, but different. A less eccentric, if equally indefensible, opinion was expressed in the 1930's by Lewis Corey, then a radical activist, when he wrote, "All that is vital in Thorstein Veblen may fulfill itself in Marxism and socialism." This of Veblen, as if he had not, at Harvard University in 1906, discussed and dismissed "The Socialist Economics of Karl Marx and His Followers" in a special series of subsequently published lectures. Veblen's critique of Marx, whose "boldness of conception and great logical consistency" he admired, is all but definitive. He branded Marx as a Romantic philosopher, committed to an inadmissible rationalism, an untenable theory of surplus value containing too many traces of David Ricardo and William Thompson, and a teleological theory of history which, through dialectic sequence, "animistically" imputed purposes and inevitability to the social process. Veblen repudiated classical economics. He felt that Marx basically belonged to that school if only by his acceptance of natural liberty and natural rights as scientific principles. Moreover, Veblen charged the latter-day socialists with having already succumbed to jingoism and militarism, an infection he thought would blight their movement as it spread from Germany to other countries. But if he was not simply a clever Marxist, what then? Some few years ago, an Englishman, reviewing The Portable Veblen, remarked that although he had never read Veblen before, the book was familiar to him because he had read Herbert Spencer as a schoolboy.

It is unlikely, shall we say, that Veblen is merely an echo of Weber (whom he did not seem to have known, though Weber knew him at least through The Theory of Business Enterprise and said so, with appreciation, in a famous footnote to The Protestant Ethic) or of Marx (so much of whose thought he explicitly rejected) or of Spencer (who was his political opposite as a champion of the system Veblen spent a lifetime abusing). Of course, he was profoundly influenced by Marx and Spencer, as he was by Charles Darwin, Immanuel Kant, William James, Jacques Loeb, Lewis Henry Morgan, Edward B. Tylor, William Graham Sumner, John Dewey, and the anonymous authors of the Icelandic sagas. No thinker, least of all one like Veblen, operates in vacuo; he borrows liberally and synthesizes freely. Montaigne, a greater genius, more given to quotation from others—in this case the ancients—put the matter in proper perspective when he defended himself as follows: "The bees plunder the flowers here and there, but afterward they make of them honey, which is all theirs; it is no longer thyme or marjoram." Veblen plundered here and there, and if what he made was more like gall than honey, it was all his.

Why does it still pay to taste that gall? Why, having sampled some, do so many of us feel stimulated and ask for more? Why, in other words, is Veblen so widely, if not always wisely, read today when he was so generally ignored in his own time? These questions occurred to me as I heard a young man in 1958 performing as the principal speaker at a symposium convoked to celebrate the centennial of Veblen's birth. This young man, on his partial reading of the texts, had found them utterly without value, an indigestible compost of error and obsolescence. Many greybeards in the audience were startled; others of us shared their reaction. Could we all have been so wrong? Well, perhaps. I had not dipped into Veblen for many years and knew only too well how perishable one's early idols can be. Veblen always seemed vulnerable to me. His several errors of fact, his occasional contradictions, his theoretical limitations, all required criticism. They stamped him as a man of his time. However, I had thought that after we put his obvious shortcomings to one side, much remained

—so much that he could also be regarded as a man of our time, and frequently as a man ahead of our time.

At any rate, I was shaken by the experience of hearing a reputable if somewhat jejune scholar state his categorical rejection of (so it seemed to me) the greatest social scientist America has produced. Accordingly, after a lapse of one decade, I reread the whole canon, all of Veblen's books and essays, spanning a period from the 1890's to his death just before the Crash of 1929. They proved to be more rewarding, more to the point, and more instructive than I had first found them. The flaws were there, and they could not be blinked away. The rest was a marvel of relevance, insight, and foresight.

Just what was it this man saw from his peculiar position in what we might call the interstitial space of contemporary mass society, perched outside, looking inside, a perpetual stranger, the marginal man par excellence? It is perhaps the manysidedness of his vision which constitutes Veblen's major contribution. But if we were pressed for a single factor to explain Veblen's relative popularity today, it would be the disenchantment of the world. Pessimism, which our forefathers of the eighteenth and nineteenth centuries found so repugnant that they would not abide its spokesmen, has all of a sudden come to be obligatory.

There are now in print inexpensive paperback and hardcover editions of The Theory of the Leisure Class, The Higher Learning, and The Theory of Business Enterprise. Veblen's thought is accessible where it was inaccessible at the time of his death. During the Great Depression, which he had foreseen, all his books were reissued. Since then, Veblen anthologies and studies have appeared in increasing number. There are no doubt many reasons for such a revival of interest. Since Veblen was a powerful writer and an extraordinary satirist, he deserves our attention on purely esthetic grounds. However, there are better writers, really creative artists, who have had to wait till the last two decades for full recognition. For example, it is only since World War II that Herman Melville, Henry James, and Henry Adams have come into their own. Why do we go back to Nathaniel Hawthorne and why do we now seek out the dark side of Huckleberry Finn when that classic previously struck us as lighthearted romance? Why, at this moment, do Kafka, Camus, Dostoyevsky—or for that matter, Freud and Nietzsche—appeal so much to the cultivated man? The question is a knotty one. I do not profess to answer it here beyond suggesting a condition common to them all. Very simply, they take a dim view of the universe, and no other view is permissible in the second half of the twentieth century.

Veblen wrote at a time when most of his contemporaries inside and outside the academy were convinced that mankind could only continue to make progress. They were prey to the deep-seated illusion of automatic and unalterable progress. The "wholesome trend" in world affairs which was so clear to such men as Adam Smith, Karl Marx, and Charles Horton Cooley—each in his own way—always remained beyond Veblen's apprehension. Where they looked to the invisible hand of Providence or the end of "prehistory" and the expropriation of capitalism as a prelude to the good classless socialist society or the infinite expansion of community values through better and better communications, Veblen clung steadily to his nightmare. For him, imbecile institutions, like national sovereignty in an economically interdependent world, stood every chance of being perpetuated. In a universe in which we are busy contaminating the atmosphere with radioactive fallout and systematically preparing for race suicide, after our experience of cataclysmic depression and global dislocation, as well as two world wars, he speaks to us and we join him in his scorn of the others.

When Sumner wrote in 1906 of his own and Veblen's era, "Such a period is one of hope, power, and gain for the masses. Optimism is the philosophy. All the mores get their spirit from it. 'Progress' is an object of faith," he encompassed not just the Victorian age as represented by Tennyson and Mill or St. Simon and Comte, but the Enlightenment which had preceded and engendered it as well. From the Founding Fathers of the Republic to the founding fathers of sociology there is a straight line of compulsive hope.

How strange for its day—and how right for ours—is Veblen's observation that "Human culture in all ages presents too many imbecile usages and principles of conduct to let anyone overlook the fact that disserviceable institutions easily arise and continue to hold their place in spite of the disapproval of native common sense." Almost everyone was able to overlook that fact. It took a peculiar stubbornness to deny what nearly everyone affirmed. Even after Veblen's death, most of us went on affirming the same shibboleth: with no sense of historical irony we billed the World's Fair of 1933, in which our gadgets were put on proud display, as "A Century of Progress." Once we learned of Belsen and Ravensbruck and as we quailed in the shadow of Hiroshima and Nagasaki, we finally ceased to speak of automatic progress.

If Condorcet as a typical philosophe believed in progress, it was because he understood man to be a rational animal, properly labeled homo sapiens. Veblen understood, without exalting, the nonrational and irrational components of human nature. The eighteenth century overestimated man's special and increasing capacity to exercise his reason. The nineteenth century, through such representative men as Herbert Spencer, erred by straining an analogy. It was, of course, the biological analogy, which in an extreme form we came to know as "organicism." Proponents of the analogy were convinced that human institutions had been made, as they would be remade and unmade, by principles governing the whole animal kingdom. These principles were set forth by Charles Darwin, and they needed only to be "applied." They were variously applied. Social Darwinism proved to be so latitudinarian a doctrine that it could encompass the conservative Spencer, who inferred from Darwin that man, like the other animals, was essentially competitive, and the anarchist Kropotkin, who inferred from Darwin that man, like the other animals, was essentially cooperative. Marx the revolutionist shared his social Darwinism with Veblen the unclassifiable iconoclast—and they shared it with the liberal Sumner, the radical Ward, the reformist Cooley, and the nationalist Giddings. Like Aristotelian philosophy, with which medieval Catholic, Jewish, and Muslim supernaturalism once had to be squared, so for some time Darwinian theory needed to be reconciled with whatever position a scholar took.

At first blush, we would have to say of Veblen that he was no exception. But how can one ever say that of Veblen? To be sure, he could think of no better way to tax economics than to charge that it was not an evolutionary science. Why not, and what of it? For Veblen, "not evolutionary" signified "static," just as "evolutionary" stood for nothing more or less than "genetic or dynamic." Smith and his followers, and even the physiocrats before them, held to an immutable model of economic man, and they frequently confounded the model with reality. Veblen found the model cumbersome and scored it for being in direct contradiction to reality. He focused attention upon monopolies, wars, and depressions, upon all those "episodes of blundering and perverse departure" from the path Smith took to be God-given. These were not mere aberrations and deviations from natural conduct; they were the stuff of social and economic life. This fact Smith, Malthus, Ricardo, Bentham, and the many others could have seen but for their tendency to describe economic activity after their hearts' desire. They wished for a state of perfect competition in which every self-seeking investor, motivated only by an acquisitive impulse, unconsciously served the commonweal. That miracle did not occur in Smith's lifetime; soon after it became a grotesque distortion.

Such, very briefly, is the nature of Veblen's indictment. He held traditional economics to be immature because its practitioners inexactly described the past and totally misrepresented the present. In a dozen brilliant essays, Veblen riddled economics for misconceiving man and failing for that reason to grow up. These essays are a consummate exercise in the sociology of knowledge; each one skillfully probes a body of ideas within the triple dimension of place, time, and society. In the end we have a persuasive critique and a cogent plea.

To some extent, the critique parallels that of Sigmund Freud in psychopathology and that of Kurt Lewin in general psychology. Lewin pointed out that physics came of age when Galileo extended scientific lawfulness from our own planet to the solar system, from earthly to heavenly matter. The Galilean attitude, in contrast with the Aristotelian, was determined by a general idea of comprehensive unity. Freud's achievement consists largely in having abolished the artificial boundary between normal and abnormal action. Lewin and his colleagues sought to attain a similar end in their assault upon established psychology: this is the basic meaning of their Gestalt or holistic or phenomenological approach to individual and small group behavior. Veblen's plea to broaden and deepen economics by conjoining it to other disciplines (notably psychology, sociology, and anthropology) is advanced in the same spirit. Both Lewin and Veblen protested against the tendency in social science to put aside apparently peculiar conditions as insusceptible of scientific analysis. Each placed particular emphasis on precisely those conditions by explaining man as a dynamic animal who had been studied for too long as a phenotype—by appearance alone—and scarcely at all as a genotype—conditionally and genetically from a standpoint much deeper than any that met the eye.

There can be no doubt that Veblen set the stage for that reconstruction of economic thought which we are now witnessing. He fructified or directly inspired a remarkable amount of work. In his book Modern Economic Thought, Allen G. Gruchy identifies Veblen as the spiritual father not only of institutional economics as it is found in his own works, but also of John R. Commons' collective economics, Wesley C. Mitchell's quantitive and social economics, John Maurice Clark's social economics, Rexford G. Tugwell's experimental economics, and Gardiner Means' administrative economics. The list could be lengthened. Veblen made an impact on the dismal science.

Whether that impact was salutary or not can only be determined from within the profession of economics—to which Veblen belonged no more than he did to any other specific sphere. Like Marx, he received his formal training in philosophy (but more in Kantian and Humean than in Hegelian philosophy, and that perhaps made all the difference); like Marx, he is commonly regarded as an economist; and, like Marx, his vocation was truly that of a sociologist. There are few men who offer us a richer legacy of understanding. With it, we can interpret our world more intelligently, formulate our hypotheses more resourcefully, and draw our inferences more meaningfully.

Sociology is hag-ridden (even now, or more so now within its dominant American school) by explorers of structural-functional stasis—to whom change occurs either as an afterthought or as a separate category to be considered apart from the present, presumably frozen situation. That model-building which excludes or minimizes change (in a period of total revolution!) should have withstood first the Marxist and then the Veblenian onslaught with their constant emphasis on process is itself a remarkable sociological fact.

We cannot apprehend the "given" unless "flux" has first been built into it. Of this, all chemists, physicists, and biologists are acutely aware. Many sociologists are not. How strange that they have turned on their own evolutionary tradition just when the material they study is becoming so mercurial as to make its analysis doubly difficult. And how necessary that we go to school to someone like Veblen. It was never more important to uphold the centrality of social change and to pursue an understanding of its laws. While we spend our time with small groups, drawing up sociometric charts and measuring artfully induced differences between "control groups" and "experimental groups," process without progress proceeds apace. Man's nature is not fixed by any necessarily transitory social configuration; neither is his destiny progressively predetermined. The air will not be cleared, and our enterprise will not prosper no matter how many shiny new instruments of inquiry we devise, until these elementary truths are re-learned. On the way back, Veblen is a useful guide.

But was not Veblen overcommitted to the anthropology of his day, that is to say, the anthropology of Morgan, Tylor, and Spencer? Yes, to some extent. One feels uneasy reading about savage and upper and lower barbarian and civilized "stages" of social development. The Spencerian pattern—from lesser to greater complexity—let alone that of his contemporaries who also saw graded stages of evolution in language, religion, and domestic relations, no longer seems to explain anything. Yet it does explain something, the one thing that most interested Veblen. It explains technology.

Tools evolve. They are simple in the beginnings of human culture. They become increasingly complex with time. No major invention has ever been lost to the species, and each one has led to others. If we look not at specific cultures, but at culture as a whole, we observe in technology precisely that process of unilinear evolution which too many social Darwinists mistakenly ascribed to all social institutions. Barring nuclear annihilation (a prospect that would not have dismayed Veblen), we may confidently assert that our technological apparatus will continue irreversibly to multiply and to increase in complexity at a constantly accelerated tempo. This is the primary datum of modern and of postmodern society.

It fascinated Veblen—and caused him to commit his only excesses. In everything he wrote there are intimations of technological determinism, always dispelled by a stronger sense of contingency and swept away completely in a masterpiece like The Higher Learning. The persistent focus on technology presented theoretical difficulties, but these were greatly outweighed by the advantages. Decades ago, with this focus, Veblen was able to perceive that:

Technology and industrial experience in large volume and at a high proficiency are indispensable to the conduct of war on the modern plan, as well as a large efficient and up-to-date industrial community and industrial plant to supply the necessary material of this warfare.

More important, he was able to anticipate what could not quite have been the case when he wrote, namely that:

The state of the industrial arts, as it bears on the peace and its violation, has been spoken of above. It is of such a character that a judiciously prepared offensive launched by any Power of the first rank at an opportune time can reach and lay waste any given country of the habitable globe.

No one would have been less surprised, or more appalled, by a further advance in destructive technology—such that the whole habitable globe and not just any given country can now be laid waste. The superficial reader of Veblen sometimes takes him to be a man who worshiped the machine, as he idealized the engineer. Yet no one understood better what horrors the machine could produce, or plunged more profoundly into the task of formulating plans to avoid them.

The war of 1914–18 stirred Veblen to a pitch of intellectual activity and emotional involvement unmatched at any other time in his life. Historians called it the Great War. We who have survived a greater war, and thresh about for ways to avoid the greatest, can only feel kinship with Veblen in his passion for peace. His was substantially the same position that Norman Angell took just before World War I. William G. Carleton has reminded us of Angell's contention that "there would be no more wars because industrialism and technology have made war too horrible and destructive for people to endure. Since then the two greatest wars in history have taken place. . . . Nevertheless, before this century is out, Norman Angell may become one of the world's true prophets. He correctly observed the trend. He miscalculated the degree of revolutionary technology and industrialization, the degree of 'total war', required to bring about the institutionalizing of peace." Most of this applies as well to Veblen, except that he did less miscalculating.

Kant had written Perpetual Peace, and Veblen's treatise The Nature of the Peace and the Terms of Its Perpetuation was consciously modeled after it. Despite its topical cast, this book, along with a companion piece, Imperial Germany and the Industrial Revolution, is altogether pertinent. Veblen's reflections on war and peace, defective and ambivalent as they sometimes are, still rivet our attention. The melancholy truth is that mankind at large has yet to learn what Veblen knew in 1915 about the causes of international conflict. Like Angell, he wrote that industrial techniques had advanced so far that no corner of the earth was secure from aggression, but unlike Angell, he foresaw that each country would react to the common menace by arming itself "defensively" against any possible attack. "Competitive preparedness" was his term for the penultimate stage of peace. For most of the past fifteen years, we have called that stage the cold war.

No Veblenian will be surprised if cold war leads to hot war in a total triumph of human imbecility. But the apocalypse could be averted. Peace might be established and preserved.

To that end, strong measures would have to be taken. In general, Veblen recommended that we promote "insubordination" among traditionally submissive peoples to help them resist propulsion into a war none of them wants; register all merchant shipping under neutral colors as a step toward the unification and pacification of mankind; instill a spirit of live and let live and of mutual succor—the Christian ethic as Veblen understood it, which, without supernatural sanction was necessary for human survival; struggle to disestablish nation-states, for their continued presence is a mischievous and obsolescent institutional arrangement—as useful in this world as the Spanish Inquisition; failing that, take measures to demilitarize and sterilize the apparatus of national life.

Is all this just opposition to sin? I suppose so. But, then, what has become of us? A conservative gentlemen like Goethe (or Goldsmith) could call himself a citizen of the world without scandalizing anyone. In our ultra-nationalistic century, patriotism (which, if it is the last refuge of a scoundrel, has made scoundrels of us all) carries more weight than common sense. A newly "radical" proposal, such as Veblen's, for the neutralization of citizenship is viewed as naively pious or dangerously delusive rhetoric. One may be sure that a hard-headed theologian like Reinhold Niebuhr would denounce it as unrealistic. Yet as Veblen argued, particularism works at cross-purposes with the economic and cultural requirements of twentieth-century society. These requirements, like science, scholarship, and art, are fundamentally cosmopolitan. No country is self-sufficient; it needs to supply other countries and to be supplied by them. To exclude one another's resources, as we do in time of crisis and tension or war, is to produce a crippling effect. Socio-economic interdependence is a fact of life, and it appeared to Veblen that patriotism (new or old, but in either case, vestigial) fitted into this scheme like dust in the eyes and sand in the bearings.

Thus, we have to do with a writer who knew the worst and usually expected it. Nothing in the superorganic, any more than in the organic or inorganic domain, was fixed forever. There is no special distinction in Veblen's opinion that "all is change" since virtually every one of his colleagues would have agreed with it. Veblen's greatest strength lies exactly where they would have demurred: in his better understanding of the direction that change would take.

Americans might have been spared their latest trauma if they had heeded this part of Veblen's message. As a people we live through breath-taking transformations and take each one of them to be final. When, a full century after Great Britain, the United States began seriously to industrialize, a whole structure of myths arose to glorify our innately superior American know-how. Finally, for a little while after 1945, and as a direct result of that know-how, world leadership —than which there is nothing more ephemeral—came to be vested ever so briefly in the United States. And this too seemed to have been in the nature of things. Then came Sputnik and shell-shock in the national psyche. Technological and political ascendancy, a revolution for which we were not prepared, seemed to be slipping quickly out of our grasp.

How so? Veblen would have explained this particular sequence of events by relating it to a general theory he had developed for the explanation of another case. The problem he set himself in 1915 was to account for the power of Germany, and, incidentally, that of Japan, another imperial state whose growth was similar to that of the kaiser reich. His solution was subtle, but it contains one very important idea which the anthropologist Ellman Service has recently appropriated with gratitude. Service calls this idea "The Law of Evolutionary Potential."

In Chapters II to IV of Imperial Germany, Veblen argues that Germany became industrially more efficient than her predecessors, England, France, Holland, and Belgium, just because she came after and borrowed from them. England paid "the penalty of taking the lead" while Germany and Japan profited from "the merits of borrowing." Belated entrance into the so-called concert of industrial nations imposes something of a handicap, but it also provides an extraordinary advantage. Germany could and did take over a ready-made technology. There was no obsolete equipment, no large capital investment in tools the continued use of which could only retard economic expansion, no conventional restrictions to hamper enterprise. When, in addition, the leaders of industry have a cheap, capable, and abundant labor supply, they have every opportunity to outdistance their rivals. Thus Veblen. Later, as Service indicates, we find the theory independently formulated by Leon Trotsky in his History of the Russian Revolution. Trotsky puts it succinctly:

Although compelled to follow after the advanced countries, a backward country does not take things in the same order. The privilege of historical backwardness—and such a privilege exists—permits, or rather compels, the adoption of whatever is ready in advance of any specified date, skipping a whole series of intermediate stages.

Veblen dealt chiefly with Germany, Trotsky with Russia, but the point they make has universal applicability. Every latecomer is advantageously situated vis-à-vis all previously industrialized powers. From this angle, there was every expectation that Soviet Russia would eclipse the productivity of England, France, Germany, and the United States. And there is now every expectation, provided we do not extinguish ourselves in the meantime, that Russia will be eclipsed by Asia, Africa, and Latin America as those slumbering giants awake. Each time the latest industrial revolution spreads to a new area, it can be absorbed with greater rapidity. Hence, the period of dominance for any one power grows shorter and shorter.

Veblen calculated that it took England six times longer than Germany to achieve industrialization. Russia, with leaders who placed all their emphasis on capital accumulation, which is to say, heavy industry, moved even faster. At present, the whole world is rushing headlong into the same vortex. Almost every nation (more so China, less so India) wishes to step up the rate of continuous economic development. How would Veblen have felt about this? He was a well-known proponent of increased production, always flailing the "captains of industry" for their obstructive tactics and supporting the engineers, those putative opponents of "the price system" who were pictured as favoring ever greater output. For all that, there were values Veblen held to be higher than economic efficiency and productivity. And these values—above all, freedom, the exercise of idle curiosity, elbowroom, self-fulfillment in creative activity—are in his judgment directly jeopardized by too rapid a rate of industrialization.

Veblen saw as well as Trotsky that there were economic advantages in late but speedy industrialization. For that boon, he also saw, as Trotsky never could, that a heavy price would have to be paid. If it creates unheard of possibilities, it also leads to unheard of dangers. Veblen described the phenomenal unfolding of German national power, pinpointed in population increase, industrial advancement, and military force. These are the components of totalitarianism, that unique combination of tyranny and technology which it has been our lot to spawn in this century. Veblen would surely have had no more stomach for Nazi Germany, Soviet Russia, or Communist China than he had for imperial Germany. Only those who adore production as an end in itself can praise any of these totalitarian systems. Veblen counted the human cost. He was revolted by gratuitous suffering and alert to new ways in which it could be inflicted upon "the underlying population."

He worried, at the same time and to our general benefit, about the upper layers of society. The specter of bureaucracy haunted him. Veblen, after all, was a visionary (as Charles Frankel recently said of John Dewey with as much justice and with the same mild sense of shock). Among the things he envisioned was what we now more fashionably call bureaucratic collectivism, the managerial or employee society, the white-collar world, and a major concomitant thereof, the organization man. Bureaucratic organization plays the central role for Veblen when he notes its presence in American universities, when he refers to trained incapacity as a major trait of business administrators, and when he contemplates the over-all pattern emerging in industrial society.

We cannot say too much for Veblen's awareness that mankind was entering an age in which, not Marx's proletariat or any other industrial working class, but the specialist, the expert, the pure and applied scientist would predominate. Automation simply fulfills the prophecy, as machines equipped with feedback begin to liquidate all forms of unskilled and semiskilled labor.

Veblen is generally remembered as an exceedingly perceptive student of social stratification, circa 1890, who invented such memorable terms as conspicuous consumption, conspicuous waste, invidious distinction, and emulation. These are valuable concepts developed in and by a free speculative spirit, transcending any one period of American history, and put sporadically to good empirical use ever since they were first set forth. Lately, sociologists have refined the class concept; some have refined it out of existence. Veblen's simple heuristic construction—the business class and the working class—may seem naive to many of them. Yet that simple construction underlay the first and best community studies: Middletown and Middletown in Transition. Veblen's two-class system evidently enables the social scientist to do better research than all the cliques, interest groups, or divided and subdivided classes have been able to inspire.

How best to stratify a society for scientific purposes remains, of course, an open question. But that society is objectively stratified into classes and will be restratified on a new basis in the future now goes without saying. We must credit Veblen with realizing that the next step would not be Marx's classless society, but still another class society, with its bureaucrats on top as the new men of power.

The things that Veblen feared, and those that most offended his moral sense, have surely materialized. We have had warfare, totalitarianism in small and large doses, bureaucracy everywhere, rampant nationalism—such that the latest "revolutionary" regime, established by Fidel Castro, has as its motto "Patria o muerte"—the triumph of trivial and commercial norms, status panic—as analyzed a few years ago by C. Wright Mills, every bit of Henry Miller's "air-conditioned nightmare"—and more, dehumanization, anxiety, and bewilderment.

Does Veblen offer mankind any way out of this extreme situation? Surely not in his half-baked scheme for a Soviet of Technicians, which was less utopian than counterutopian and in which he had no real confidence himself. By his devotion to science? But even this would not be "constructive" for, although his philosophy of science—pragmatic, provisional, probabilistic, and modest—is substantially the same as that which most men of science respect today, it points to the limitations of science and away from "scientism." Veblen was forever pointing to limitations, forever ridiculing the deification of ideas. He was a chronic complainer. He criticized, he deflated, he satirized savagely. Given the inherently imperfect nature of any society, it is unimaginable that he should ever have assumed any other role. Our imperfections at this moment threaten to wipe out civilization. Therefore, it may well be that the deepest lesson we can learn from Veblen is to emulate his perpetual discontent. If enough of us were fired by his kind of dissent, if we could rouse ourselves from the torpor of complaisance by vigorous nay-saying, if we too could become professional "cranks," never satisfied with things as they are, then we might help mankind to survive.

1

The Theory of Business Enterprise*

Veblen was at the height of his scholarly and satirical powers when he sat down, more than half a century ago, to write The Theory of Business Enterprise. He had already polished his comic style and his tragic vision to a fine point of acuity. They inform this, his most technical, influential, and hilarious work. The familiar themes, especially those that stem from Veblen's basic distinction between industrial and pecuniary activity, are to be found here. So is a large measure of how we live now.

The price system against which Veblen argued with such savagery distressed him most because of its parasitism. The term "parasitism" meant many things to him, among them "conspicuous waste" and "conspicuous consumption." It also implied depersonalization and alienation. Above all, in his own terms, it suggested that men, once they gave up handicraft production, were systematically deflected from what he took to be their innate "instinct of workmanship." The loss of old creative satisfactions left a void that cash value and material comfort could not completely fill.

But in the selection that follows, Veblen is more explicit about parasitism. He means advertising and war. He means and explains marginal differentiation, a technique by which advertisers promote the illusion of difference among variously labeled but actually identical products. The significance of packaging and brand loyalty and built-in obsolescence did not escape him. He would have saluted the economy of the 1960's with as much respect as he showed for "the

* From *The Theory of Business Enterprise* (New York: Charles Scribner's Sons, 1904), pp. 41–65.

price system" in 1908. We now average $12 million per annum on advertising expenditures in the United States. And in 1960 the late Dag Hammerskjold, Secretary-General of the United Nations, estimated that $320 million a day or nearly $117 billion a year was being spent on armaments around the world. The figure is indeterminately higher today. It alone justifies Veblen's worst forebodings.

In current economic theory the business man is spoken of under the name of "entrepreneur" or "undertaker," and his function is held to be the coördinating of industrial processes with a view to economies of production and heightened serviceability. The soundness of this view need not be questioned. It has a great sentimental value and is useful in many ways. There is also a modicum of truth in it as an account of facts. In common with other men, the business man is moved by ideals of serviceability and an aspiration to make the way of life easier for his fellows. Like other men, he has something of the instinct of workmanship. No doubt such aspirations move the great business man less urgently than many others, who are, on that account, less successful in business affairs. Motives of this kind detract from business efficiency, and an undue yielding to them on the part of business men is to be deprecated as an infirmity. Still, throughout men's dealings with one another and with the interests of the community there runs a sense of equity, fair dealing, and workmanlike integrity; and in an uncertain degree this bent discountenances gain that is got at an undue cost to others, or without rendering some colorable equivalent. Business men are also, in a measure, guided by the ambition to effect a creditable improvement in the industrial processes which their business traffic touches. These sentimental factors in business exercise something of a constraint, varying greatly from one person to another, but not measurable in its aggregate results. The careers of most of the illustrious business men show the presence of some salutary constraint of this kind. Not infrequently an excessive sensitiveness of this kind leads to a withdrawal from business, or from certain forms of business which may appeal to a vivid fancy as peculiarly dishonest or peculiarly detrimental to the community.[1] Such grounds of action, and perhaps others equally

[1] Illustrative instances will readily suggest themselves. Many a business man turns by preference to something less dubious than the distilling of whiskey or the sale of deleterious household remedies. They prefer not to use deleterious adulterants, even within the limits of the law. They will rather use wool than shoddy at the

genial and equally unbusinesslike, would probably be discovered by a detailed scrutiny of any large business deal. Probably in many cases the business strategist, infected with this human infirmity, reaches an agreement with his rivals and his neighbors in the industrial system without exacting the last concession that a ruthless business strategy might entitle him to. The result is, probably, a speedier conclusion and a smoother working of the large coalitions than would follow from the unmitigated sway of business principles.[2]

But the sentiment which in this way acts in constraint of business traffic proceeds on such grounds of equity and fair dealing as are afforded by current business ethics; it acts within the range of business principles, not in contravention of them; it acts as a conventional restraint upon pecuniary advantage, not in abrogation of it. This code of business ethics consists, after all, of mitigations of the maxim, *Caveat emptor*. It touches primarily the dealings of man with man, and only less directly and less searchingly inculcates temperance and circumspection as regards the ulterior interests of the community at large. Where this moral need of a balance between the services rendered the community and the gain derived from a given business transaction asserts itself at all, the balance is commonly sought to be maintained in some sort of pecuniary terms; but pecuniary terms afford only a very inadequate measure of serviceability to the community.

Great and many are the items of service to be set down to the business man's account in connection with the organization of the industrial system, but when all is said, it is still to be kept in mind that his work in the correlation of industrial processes is chiefly of

same price. The officials of a railway commonly prefer to avoid wrecks and manslaughter, even if there is no pecuniary advantage in choosing the more humane course. More than that, it will be found true that the more prosperous of the craft, especially, take pride and pains to make the service of their roads or the output of their mills as efficient, not simply as the pecuniary advantage of the concern demands, but as the best pecuniary results will admit. Instances are perhaps not frequent, but they are also not altogether exceptional, where a prosperous captain of industry will go out of his way to heighten the serviceability of his industry even to a degree that is of doubtful pecuniary expediency for himself. Such aberrations are, of course, not large; and if they are persisted in to any very appreciable extent the result is, of course, disastrous to the enterprise. The enterprise in such a case falls out of the category of business management and falls under the imputation of philanthropy.

[2] The captains of the first class necessarily are relatively exempt from these unbusinesslike scruples.

a permissive kind. His furtherance of industry is at the second remove, and is chiefly of a negative character. In his capacity as business man he does not go creatively into the work of perfecting mechanical processes and turning the means at hand to new or larger uses. That is the work of the men who have in hand the devising and oversight of mechanical processes. The men in industry must first create the mechanical possibility of such new and more efficient methods and correlations, before the business man sees the chance, makes the necessary business arrangements, and gives general directions that the contemplated industrial advance shall go into effect. The period between the time of earliest practicability and the effectual completion of a given consolidation in industry marks the interval by which the business man retards the advance of industry. Against this are to be offset the cases, comparatively slight and infrequent, where the business men in control push the advance of industry into new fields and prompt the men concerned with the mechanics of the case to experiment and exploration in new fields of mechanical process.

When the recital is made, therefore, of how the large consolidations take place at the initiative of the business men who are in control, it should be added that the fact of their being in control precludes industrial correlations from taking place except by their advice and consent. The industrial system is organized on business principles and for pecuniary ends. The business man is at the centre; he holds the discretion and he exercises it freely, and his choice falls out now on one side, now on the other. The retardation as well as the advance is to be set down to his account.

As regards the economies in cost of production effected by these consolidations, there is a further characteristic feature to be noted, a feature of some significance for any theory of modern business. In great measure the saving effected is a saving of the costs of business management and of the competitive costs of marketing products and services, rather than a saving in the prime costs of production. The heightened facility and efficiency of the new and larger business combinations primarily affect the expenses of office work and sales, and it is in great part only indirectly that this curtailment and consolidation of business management has an effect upon the methods and aims of industry proper. It touches the pecuniary processes immediately, and the mechanical processes indirectly and in an uncertain degree. It is of the nature of a partial neutralization of the wastes due to the presence of pecuniary motives and business management,—for the business management involves waste wherever a greater number of men or transactions are involved than are necessary to the effective direction of the mechanical processes employed. The amount of "business" that has to be transacted per unit of product is much greater where the various related industrial processes are managed in severalty than where several of them are brought under one business management. A pecuniary discretion has to be exercised at every point of contact or transition, where the process or its product touches or passes the boundary between different spheres of ownership. Business transactions have to do with ownership and changes of ownership. The greater the parcelment in point of ownership, the greater the amount of business work that has to be done in connection with a given output of goods or services, and the slower, less facile, and less accurate, on the whole, is the work. This applies both to the work of bargain and contract, wherein pecuniary initiative and discretion are chiefly exercised, and to the routine work of accounting, and of gathering and applying information and misinformation.

The standardization of industrial processes, products, services, and consumers, spoken of in an earlier chapter, very materially facilitates the business man's work in reorganizing business enterprises on a larger scale; particularly does this standardization serve his ends by permitting a uniform routine in accounting, invoices, contracts, etc., and so admitting a large central accounting system, with homogeneous ramifications, such as will give a competent conspectus of the pecuniary situation of the enterprise at any given time.

The great, at the present stage of development perhaps the greatest, opportunity for saving by consolidation, in the common run of cases, is afforded by the ubiquitous and in a sense excessive presence of business enterprise in the economic system. It is in doing away with unnecessary business transactions and industrially futile manœuvring on the part of independent firms that the promoter of combinations finds his most telling opportunity. So that it is scarcely an overstatement to say that probably the largest, assuredly the securest and most unquestionable, service rendered by the great modern captains of industry is this curtailment of the business to be done,—this sweeping retirement of business men as a class from the service and the definitive cancelment of opportunities for private enterprise.

So long as related industrial units are under different business managements, they are, by the nature of the case, at cross-purposes, and business consolidation remedies this untoward feature of the industrial system by eliminating the pecuniary element from the interstices of the system as far as may be. The interstitial adjustments of the industrial system at large are in this way withdrawn from the discretion of rival business men, and the work of pecuniary management previously involved is in large part dispensed with, with the result that there is a saving of work and an avoidance of that systematic mutual hindrance that characterizes the competitive management of industry. To the community at large the work of pecuniary management, it appears, is less serviceable the more there is of it. The heroic rôle of the captain of industry is that of a deliverer from an excess of business management. It is a casting out of business men by the chief of business men.

The theory of business enterprise sketched above applies to such business as is occupied with the interstitial adjustments of the system of industries. This work of keeping and of disturbing the interstitial adjustments does not look immediately to the output of goods as its source of gain, but to the alterations of values involved in disturbances of the balance, and to the achievement of a more favorable business situation for some of the enterprises engaged. This work lies in the middle, between commercial enterprise proper, on the one hand, and industrial enterprise in the stricter sense, on the other hand. It is directed to the acquisition of gain through taking advantage of those conjunctures of business that arise out of the concatenation of processes in the industrial system.

In a similar manner commercial business may be said to be occupied with conjunctures that arise out of the circumstances of the industrial system at large, but not originating in the mechanical exigencies of the industrial processes. The conjunctures of commercial business proper are in the main fortuitous, in so far that they are commonly not initiated by the business men engaged in these commercial pursuits. Commercial business, simply as such, does not aim to guide the course of industry.

On the other hand, the large business enterprise spoken of above initiates changes in industrial organization and seeks its gain in large part through such alterations of value levels as take place on its own initiative. These alterations of the value levels, of course, have their effect upon the output of goods and upon the material welfare of the community; but the effect which they have in this way is only incidental to the quest of profits.

But apart from this remoter and larger guidance of the course of industry, the business men also, and more persistently and pervasively, exercise a guidance over the course of industry in detail. The production of goods and services is carried on for gain, and the output of goods is controlled by business men with a view to gain. Commonly, in ordinary routine business, the gains come from this output of goods and services. By the sale of the output the business man in industry "realizes" his gains. To "realize" means to convert salable goods into money values. The sale is the last step in the process and the end of the business man's endeavor. When he has disposed of the output, and so has converted his holdings of consumable articles into money values, his gains are as nearly secure and definitive as the circumstances of modern life admit. It is in terms of price that he keeps his accounts, and in the same terms he computes his output of products. The vital point of production with him is the vendibility of the output, its convertibility into money values, not its serviceability for the needs of mankind. A modicum of serviceability, for some purpose or other, the output must have if it is to be salable. But it does not follow that the highest serviceability gives the largest gains to the business man in terms of money, nor does it follow that the output need in all cases have other than a factitious serviceability. There is, on the one hand, such a possibility as overstocking the market with any given line of goods, to the detriment of the business man concerned, but not necessarily to the immediate disadvantage of the body of consumers. And there are, on the other hand, certain lines of industry, such as many advertising enterprises, the output of which may be highly effective for its purpose but of quite equivocal use to the community. Many well-known and prosperous enterprises which advertise and sell patent medicines and other proprietary articles might be cited in proof.

In the older days, when handicraft was the rule of the industrial system, the personal contact between the producer and his customer was somewhat close and lasting. Under these circumstances the factor of personal esteem and disesteem had a considerable play in controlling the purveyors of goods and services. This factor of personal contact counted in two divergent ways: (1) producers were careful of their reputation for workmanship, even apart from the gains which such a reputation might bring; and (2) a degree of irritation and ill-will would arise in many cases, leading to petty trade quarrels and discriminations on other grounds than the gains to be got, at the same time that the detail character of dealings between producer and consumer admitted a degree of petty knavery and huckstering that is no longer practicable in the current large-scale business dealings. Of these two divergent effects resulting from close personal relations between producer and consumer the former seems on the whole to have been of preponderant consequence. Under the system of handicraft and neighborhood industry, the adage that "Honesty is the best policy" seems on the whole to have been accepted and to have been true. This adage has come down from the days before the machine's régime and before modern business enterprise.

Under modern circumstances, where industry is carried on on a large scale, the discretionary head of an industrial enterprise is commonly removed from all personal contact with the body of customers for whom the industrial process under his control purveys goods or services. The mitigating effect which personal contact may have in dealings between man and man is therefore in great measure eliminated. The whole takes on something of an impersonal character. One can with an easier conscience and with less of a sense of meanness take advantage of the necessities of people whom one knows of only as an indiscriminate aggregate of consumers. Particularly is this true when, as frequently happens in the modern situation, this body of consumers belongs in the main to another, inferior class, so that personal contact and cognizance of them is not only not contemplated, but is in a sense impossible. Equity, in excess of the formal modicum specified by law, does not so readily assert its claims where the relations between the parties are remote and impersonal as where one is dealing with one's necessitous neighbors who live on the same social plane. Under these circumstances the adage cited above loses much of its axiomatic force. Business management has a chance to proceed on a temperate and sagacious calculation of profit and loss, untroubled by sentimental considerations of human kindness or irritation or of honesty.

The broad principle which guides producers and merchants, large and small, in fixing the prices at which they offer their wares and services is what is known in the language of the railroads as "charging what the traffic will bear." Where a given enterprise has a strict monopoly of the supply of a given article or of a given class of services this principle applies in the unqualified form in which it has been understood among those who discuss railway charges. But where the monopoly is less strict, where there are competitors, there the competition that has to be met is one of the factors to be taken account of in determining what the traffic will bear; competition may even become the most serious factor in the case if the enterprise in question has little or none of the character of a monopoly. But it is very doubtful if there are any successful business ventures within the range of the modern industries from which the monopoly element is wholly absent.[3] They are, at any rate, few and not of great magnitude. And the endeavor of all such enterprises that look to a permanent continuance of their business is to establish as much of a monopoly as may be. Such a monopoly position may be a legally established one, or one due to location or the control of natural resources, or it may be a monopoly of a less definite character resting on custom and prestige (good-will). This latter class of monopolies are not commonly classed as such; although in character and degree the advantage which they give is very much the same as that due to a differential advantage in location or in the command of resources. The end sought by the systematic advertising of the larger business concerns is such a monopoly of custom and prestige. This form of monopoly is sometimes of great value, and is frequently sold under the name of good-will, trade-marks, brands, etc. Instances are known where such monopolies of custom, prestige, prejudice, have been sold at prices running up into the millions.[4]

The great end of consistent advertising is to establish such differential monopolies resting on popular conviction. And the advertiser is successful in this endeavor to establish a profitable popular conviction, somewhat in proportion as he correctly apprehends the manner in which a popular conviction on any given topic is built up.[5] The

[3] "Monopoly" is here used in that looser sense which it has colloquially, not in the strict sense of an exclusive control of the supply. . . .

[4] *E.g.* the prestige value of Ivory Soap.

[5] . . . The writing and designing of advertisements (letterpress, display, and illustrations) has grown into a distinct calling; so that the work of a skilled writer of advertisements compares not unfavorably, in point of lucrativeness, with that of the avowed writers of popular fiction.

The psychological principles of advertising may be formulated somewhat as follows: A declaration of fact, made in the form and with the incidents of taste and expression to which a person is accustomed, will be accepted as authentic and will be acted upon if occasion arises, in so far as it does not conflict with opinions already accepted. The acceptance of an opinion seems to be almost entirely a passive matter. The presumption remains in favor of an opinion that has once been accepted, and an appreciable burden of proof falls on the negative. A competent formulation of opinion on a given point is the chief factor in gaining

cost, as well as the pecuniary value and the magnitude, of this organized fabrication of popular convictions is indicated by such statements as that the proprietors of a certain well-known household remedy, reputed among medical authorities to be of entirely dubious value, have for a series of years found their profits in spending several million dollars annually in advertisements. This case is by no means unique.

It has been said, no doubt in good faith and certainly with some reason, that advertising as currently carried on gives the body of consumers valuable information and guidance as to the ways and means whereby their wants can be satisfied and their purchasing power can be best utilized. To the extent to which this holds true, advertising is a service to the community. But there is a large reservation to be made on this head. Advertising is competitive; the greater part of it aims to divert purchases, etc., from one channel to another

---

adherents to that opinion, and a reiteration of the statement is the chief factor in carrying conviction. The truth of such a formulation is a matter of secondary consequence, but a wide and patent departure from known fact generally weakens its persuasive effect. The aim of the advertiser is to arrest attention and then present his statement in such a manner that it is easily assimilated into the habits of thought of the person whose conviction is to be influenced. When this is effectually done a reversal of the conviction so established is a matter of considerable difficulty. The tenacity of a view once accepted in this way is evidenced, for instance, by the endless number and variety of testimonials to the merits of well-advertised but notoriously worthless household remedies and the like.

So acute an observer as Mr. Sombart is still able to hold the opinion that "auf Schwindel ist dauernd noch nie ein Unternehmen begründet worden" (*Kapitalismus,* vol. II. p. 376). Mr. Sombart has not made acquaintance with the adventures of Elijah the Restorer, nor is he conversant with American patent-medicine enterprise. With Mr. Sombart's view may be contrasted that of Mr. L. F. Ward, an observer of equally large outlook and acumen:—

"The law of mind as it operates in society as an aid to competition and in the interest of the individual is essentially immoral. It rests primarily on the principle of deception. It is an extension to other human beings of the method applied to the animal world by which the latter was subjected to man. This method was that of the ambush and the snare. Its ruling principle was cunning. Its object was to deceive, circumvent, ensnare, and capture. Low animal cunning was succeeded by more refined kinds of cunning. The more important of these go by the names of business shrewdness, strategy, and diplomacy, none of which differ from ordinary cunning in anything but the degree of adroitness by which the victim is outwitted. In this way social life is completely honeycombed with deception."—"The Psychologic Basis of Social Economics," *Ann. of Am. Acad.,* vol. III, pp. 83–84 [475–476].

channel of the same general class.[6] And to the extent to which the efforts of advertising in all its branches are spent on this competitive disturbance of trade, they are, on the whole, of slight if any immediate service to the community. Such advertising, however, is indispensable to most branches of modern industry; but the necessity of most of the advertising is not due to its serving the needs of the community nor to any aggregate advantage accruing to the concerns which advertise, but to the fact that a business concern which falls short in advertising fails to get its share of trade. Each concern must advertise, chiefly because the others do. The aggregate expenditure that could advantageously be put into advertising in the absence of competition would undoubtedly be but an inconsiderable fraction of what is actually incurred, and necessarily incurred under existing circumstances.

Not all advertising is wholly competitive, or at least it is not always obviously so. In proportion as an enterprise has secured a monopoly position, its advertising loses the air of competitive selling and takes on the character of information designed to increase the use of its output independently. But such an increase implies a redistribution of consumption on the part of the customers. So that the element of competitive selling is after all not absent in these cases, but takes the form of competition between different classes of wares instead of competitive selling of different brands of the same class of wares.

Attention is here called to this matter of advertising and the necessity of it in modern competitive business for the light which it throws on "cost of production" in the modern system, where the process of production is under the control of business men and is carried on for business ends. Competitive advertising is an unavoidable item in the aggregate costs of industry. It does not add to the serviceability of the output, except it be incidentally and unintentionally. What it aims at is the sale of the output, and it is for this purpose that it is useful. It gives vendibility, which is useful to the seller, but has no utility to the last buyer. Its ubiquitous presence in the costs of any business enterprise that has to do with the production of goods for the market enforces the statement that the "cost of production" of commodities under the modern business system is cost incurred

[6] Advertising and other like expedients for the sale of goods aim at changes in the "substitution values" of the goods in question, not at an enhancement of the aggregate utilities of the available output of goods.

with a view to vendibility, not with a view to serviceability of the goods for human use.

There is, of course, much else that goes into the cost of competitive selling, besides the expenses of advertising, although advertising may be the largest and most unequivocal item to be set down to that account. A great part of the work done by merchants and their staff of employees, both wholesale and retail, as well as by sales-agents not exclusively connected with any one mercantile house, belongs under the same head. Just how large a share of the costs of the distribution of goods fairly belongs under the rubric of competitive selling can of course not be made out. It is largest, on the whole, in the case of consumable goods marketed in finished form for the consumer, but there is more or less of it throughout. The goods turned out on a large scale by the modern industrial processes, on the whole, carry a larger portion of such competitive costs than the goods still produced by the old-fashioned detail methods of handicraft and household industry; although this distinction does not hold hard and fast. In some extreme cases the cost of competitive selling may amount to more than ninety per cent. of the total cost of the goods when they reach the consumer. In other lines of business, commonly occupied with the production of staple goods, this constituent of cost may perhaps fall below ten per cent. of the total. Where the average, for the price of finished goods delivered to the consumers, may lie would be a hazardous guess.[7]

It is evident that the gains which accrue from this business of competitive selling and buying bear no determinable relation to the services which the work in question may render the community. If a comparison may be hazarded between two unknown and indeterminate quantities, it may perhaps be said that the gains from competitive selling bear something more of a stable relation to the service rendered than do the gains derived from speculative transactions or from the financiering operations of the great captains of industry. It seems at least safe to say that the converse will not hold true. Gains and services seem more widely out of touch in the case of the large-scale financiering work. Not that the work of the large business men in

[7] Where competitive selling makes up a large proportion of the aggregate final cost of the marketed product, this fact is likely to show itself in an exceptionally large proportion of good-will in the capitalization of the concerns engaged in the given line of business; as, *e.g.*, the American Chicle Company.

reorganizing and consolidating the industrial process is of slight consequence; but as a general proposition, the amount of the business man's gains from any given transaction of this latter class bear no traceable relation to any benefit which the community may derive from the transaction.

As to the wages paid to the men engaged in the routine of competitive selling, as salesmen, buyers, accountants, and the like,—much the same holds true of them as of the income of the business men who carry on the business on their own initiative. Their employers pay the wages of these persons, not because their work is productive of benefit to the community, but because it brings a gain to the employers. The point to which the work is directed is profitable sales, and the wages are in some proportion to the efficiency of this work as counted in terms of heightened vendibility.

The like holds true for the work and pay of the force of workmen engaged in the industrial processes under business management. It holds, in a measure, of all modern industry that produces for the market, but it holds true, in an eminent degree, of those lines of industry that are more fully under the guidance of modern business methods. These are most closely in touch with the market and are most consistently guided by considerations of vendibility. They are also, on the whole, more commonly carried on by hired labor, and the wages paid are competitively adjusted on grounds of the vendibility of the product. The brute serviceability of the output of these industries may be a large factor in its vendibility, perhaps the largest factor; but the fact remains that the end sought by the business men in control is a profitable sale, and the wages are paid as a means to that end, not to the end that the way of life may be smoother for the ultimate consumer of the goods produced.[8]

The outcome of this recital, then, is that wherever and in so far as business ends and methods dominate modern industry the relation

[8] It might, therefore, be feasible to set up a theory to the effect that wages are competitively proportioned to the vendibility of the product; but there is no cogent ground for saying that the wages in any department of industry, under a business régime, are proportioned to the utility which the output has to any one else than the employer who sells it. When it is further taken into account that the vendibility of the product in very many lines of production depends chiefly on the wastefulness of the goods (cf. *Theory of the Leisure Class*, ch. V.), the divergence between the usefulness of the work and the wages paid for it seems wide enough to throw the whole question of an equivalence between work and pay out of theoretical consideration. . . .

between the usefulness of the work (for other purposes than pecuniary gain) and the remuneration of it is remote and uncertain to such a degree that no attempt at formulating such a relation is worth while. This is eminently and obviously true of the work and gains of business men, in whatever lines of business they are engaged. This follows as a necessary consequence of the nature of business management.

Work that is, on the whole, useless or detrimental to the community at large may be as gainful to the business man and to the workmen whom he employs as work that contributes substantially to the aggregate livelihood. This seems to be peculiarly true of the bolder flights of business enterprise. In so far as its result are not detrimental to human life at large, such unproductive work directed to securing an income may seem to be an idle matter in which the rest of the community has no substantial interests. Such is not the case. In so far as the gains of these unproductive occupations are of a substantial character, they come out of the aggregate product of the other occupations in which the various classes of the community engage. The aggregate profits of the business, whatever its character, are drawn from the aggregate output of goods and services; and whatever goes to the maintenance of the profits of those who contribute nothing substantial to the output is, of course, deducted from the income of the others, whose work tells substantially.

There are, therefore, limits to the growth of the industrially parasitic lines of business just spoken of. A disproportionate growth of parasitic industries, such as most advertising and much of the other efforts that go into competitive selling, as well as warlike expenditure and other industries directed to turning out goods for conspicuously wasteful consumption, would lower the effective vitality of the community to such a degree as to jeopardize its chances of advance or even its life. The limits which the circumstances of life impose in this respect are of a selective character, in the last resort. A persistent excess of parasitic and wasteful efforts over productive industry must bring on a decline. But owing to the very high productive efficiency of the modern mechanical industry, the margin available for wasteful occupations and wasteful expenditures is very great. The requirements of the aggregate livelihood are so far short of the possible output of goods by modern methods as to leave a very wide margin for waste and parasitic income. So that instances of such a decline, due to industrial exhaustion, drawn from the history of any earlier phase of economic life, carry no well-defined lesson as to what a modern industrial community may allow itself in this respect.

While it is in the nature of things unavoidable that the management of industry by modern business methods should involve a large misdirection of effort and a very large waste of goods and services, it is also true that the aims and ideals to which this manner of economic life gives effect act forcibly to offset all this incidental futility. These pecuniary aims and ideals have a very great effect, for instance, in making men work hard and unremittingly, so that on this ground alone the business system probably compensates for any wastes involved in its working. There seems, therefore, to be no tenable ground for thinking that the working of the modern business system involves a curtailment of the community's livelihood. It makes up for its wastefulness by the added strain which it throws upon those engaged in the productive work.

2

The Higher Learning in America*

From his earliest days as a student—first at Carleton College, then at Yale and Cornell—and for the rest of his active life as a professor, Veblen lived in an academic environment. That environment was an integral part of the larger society whose values he could not accept, even though his chosen environment was also presumed to cherish higher values which he did accept with a passion. The higher values, the legitimate purposes of education, were those of science and scholarship, the disinterested pursuit of knowledge, the exercise of idle curiosity (wherever it might lead and for no ulterior or pragmatic purpose).

He saw little hope for an educational establishment that was distracted from its only legitimate purposes, and he saw it being so distracted on every side. Religion had finally withdrawn from a position of dominance in the academy, only to be replaced by business. One seemed to him to be as much an impediment and as great a drain as the other. There were no limits to his exasperation or his despair: he considered calling his treatise on The Higher Learning in America *"A Study in Total Depravity."*

If the following brief selection from that book rings a bell, it is perhaps because one hears so many reverberations of it in contemporary literature. For we live at a time when everyone knows the cash value of a B.A., when schools of commerce burgeon as their spirit spreads to every area of education, while learning for its own sake is more than ever eclipsed by extraneous military and economic preoccupations.

* From Thorstein Veblen, *The Higher Learning in America,* pp. 200–210. Copyright 1918 by B. W. Huebsch, 1946 by Ann B. Sims. Reprinted by permission of The Viking Press, Inc.

. . . . The man of the world—that is to say, of the business world—puts the question, What is the use of this learning? and the men who speak for learning, and even the scholars occupied with the "humanities," are at pains to find some colourable answer that shall satisfy the worldly-wise that this learning for which they speak is in some way useful for pecuniary gain.[1]

If he were not himself infected with the pragmatism of the market-place, the scholar's answer would have to be: Get thee behind me!

Benjamin Franklin—high-bred pragmatist that he was—once put away such a question with the rejoinder: What is the use of a baby? To civilized men—with the equivocal exception of the warlike politicians—this latter question seems foolish, criminally foolish. But there once was a time, in the high days of barbarism, when thoughtful men were ready to canvass that question with as naïve a gravity as this other question, of the use of learning, is canvassed by the substantial citizens of the present day. At the period covered by that chapter in ancient history, a child was, in a way, an article of equipment for the up-keep of the family and its prestige, and more remotely for the support of the sovereign and his prestige. So that a male child would be rated as indubitably worth while if he gave promise of growing into a robust and contentious man. If the infant were a girl, or if he gave no promise of becoming an effective disturber of the peace, the use or expediency of rearing the child would become a matter for deliberation; and not infrequently the finding of those old-time utilitarians was adverse, and the investment was cancelled. The habit of so deliberating on the pragmatic advisability of child-life has been lost, latterly; or at any rate such of the latterday utilitarians as may still entertain a question of this kind in any concrete case are ashamed to have it spoken of nakedly. Witness the lame but irrepressible sentimental protest against the Malthusian doctrine of population.

It is true, in out-of-the-way corners and on the lower levels—and on the higher levels of imperial politics—where men have not learned to shrink from shameful devices, the question of children and of the

[1] So, a man eminent as a scholar and in the social sciences has said, not so long ago: "The first question I would ask is, has not this learning a large part to play in supplementing those practical powers, instincts and sympathies which can be developed only in action, only through experience? . . . That broader training is just what is needed by the higher and more responsible ranks of business, both private and public. . . . Success in large trading has always needed breadth of view."

birth-rate is still sometimes debated as a question of the presumptive use of offspring for some ulterior end. And there may still be found those who are touched by the reflection that a child born may become a valuable asset as a support for the parents' old age. Such a pecuniary rating of the parental relation, which values children as a speculative means of gain, may still be met with. But wherever modern civilization has made its way at all effectually, such a provident rating of offspring is not met with in good company. Latterday common sense does not countenance it.

Not that a question of expediency is no longer entertained, touching this matter of children, but it is no longer the patriarchal-barbarian question as to eventual gains that may be expected to accrue to the parent or the family. Except in the view of those statesmen of the barbarian line who see the matter of birth-rate from the higher ground of dynastic politics, a child born is not rated as a means, but as an end. At least conventionally, it is no longer a question of pecuniary gain for the parent but of expediency for the child. No mother asks herself if her child will pay.

Civilized men shrink from anything like rating children as a contrivance for use in the "round-about process of the production of goods." And in much the same spirit, and in the last analysis on much the same grounds, although in a less secure and more loosely speculative fashion, men also look to the higher learning as the ripe fulfilment of material competency, rather than as a means to material success. In their thoughtful intervals, the most businesslike pragmatists will avow such an ideal. But in workday detail, when the question turns concretely on the advisability of the higher education, the workday habit of pecuniary traffic asserts itself, and the matter is then likely to be argued in pecuniary terms. The barbarian animus, habitual to the quest of gain, reverts, and the deliberation turns on the gainfulness of this education, which has in all sobriety been acknowledged the due end of culture and endeavour. So that, in working out the details, this end of living is made a means, and the means is made an end.

No doubt, what chiefly urges men to the pursuit of knowledge is their native bent of curiosity,—an impulsive proclivity to master the logic of facts; just as the chief incentive to the achievement of children has, no doubt, always been the parental bent. But very much as the boorish element in the present and recent generations will let the pecuniary use of children come in as a large subsidiary ground of decision, and as they have even avowed this to be their chief concern in the matter; so, in a like spirit, men trained to the business system of competitive gain and competitive spending will not be content to find that they can afford the quest of that knowledge which their human propensity incites them to cultivate, but they must back this propensity with a shamefaced apology for education on the plea of its gainfulness.

What is here said of the businesslike spirit of the latterday "educators" is not to be taken as reflecting disparagingly on them or their endeavours. They respond to the call of the times as best they can. That they do so, and that the call of the times is of this character, is a fact of the current drift of things; which one may commend or deprecate according as one has the fortune to fall in with one or the other side of the case; that is to say according to one's habitual bent; but in any event it is to be taken as a fact of the latterday situation, and a factor of some force and permanence in the drift of things academic, for the present and the calculable future. It means a more or less effectual further diversion of interest and support from science and scholarship to the competitive acquisition of wealth, and therefore also to its competitive consumption. Through such a diversion of energy and attention in the schools, the pecuniary animus at large, and pecuniary standards of worth and value, stand to gain, more or less, at the cost of those other virtues that are, by the accepted tradition of modern Christendom, held to be of graver and more enduring import. It means an endeavour to substitute the pursuit of gain and expenditure in place of the pursuit of knowledge, as the focus of interest and the objective end in the modern intellectual life.

This incursion of pecuniary ideals in academic policy is seen at its broadest and baldest in the Schools of Commerce,—"Commerce and Politics," "Business Training," "Commerce and Administration," "Commerce and Finance," or whatever may be the phrase selected to designate the supersession of learning by worldly wisdom. Facility in competitive business is to take the place of scholarship, as the goal of university training, because, it is alleged, the former is the more useful. The ruling interest of Christendom, in this view, is pecuniary gain. And training for commercial management stands to this ruling interest of the modern community in a relation analogous to that in which theology and homiletics stood to the ruling interest in those earlier times when the salvation of men's souls was the prime object of solicitude. Such a seminary of business has something of a sacerdotal dignity. It is the appointed keeper of the higher business animus.[2]

Such a school, with its corps of instructors and its equipment, stands in the university on a tenure similar to that of the divinity school. Both schools are equally extraneous to that "intellectual enterprise" in behalf of which, ostensibly, the university is maintained. But while the divinity school belongs to the old order and is losing its preferential hold on the corporation of learning, the school of commerce belongs to the new order and is gaining ground. The primacy among pragmatic interests has passed from religion to business, and the school of commerce is the exponent and expositor of this primacy. It is the perfect flower of the secularization of the universities. And as has already been remarked above, there is also a wide-sweeping movement afoot to bend the ordinary curriculum of the higher schools to the service of this cult of business principles, and so to make the ordinary instruction converge to the advancement of business enterprise, very much as it was once dutifully arranged that the higher instruction should be subservient to religious teaching and consonant with the demands of devout observances and creeds.

It is not that the College of Commerce stands alone as the exponent of worldly wisdom in the modern universities; nor is its position in this respect singular, except in the degree of its remoteness from all properly academic interests. Other training schools, as in engineering and in the other professions, belong under the same general category of practical aims, as contrasted with the aims of the higher learning. But the College of Commerce stands out pre-eminent among these various training schools in two respects: (a) While the great proportion of training for the other professions draws largely on the results of modern science for ways and means, and therefore includes or presumes a degree of familiarity with the work, aims and methods of the sciences, so that these schools have so much of a bond of community with the higher learning, the school of commerce on

[2] Cf., e.g., Report of a *Conference on Commercial Education and Business Progress:* In connection with the dedication of the Commerce Building, at the University of Illinois, 1913. The somewhat raucous note of self-complacency that pervades this characteristic document should not be allowed to lessen its value as evidence of the spirit for which it speaks. Indeed, whatever it may show, of effrontery and disingenuousness, is rather to be taken as of the essence of the case. It might prove difficult to find an equally unabashed pronouncement of the like volume and consistency put forth under the like academic auspices; but it does by no means stand alone, and its perfections should not be counted against it.

the other hand need scarcely take cognizance of the achievements of science, nor need it presume any degree of acquaintance on the part of its students or adepts with the matter or logic of the sciences;[3] (b) in varying degrees, the proficiency given by training in the other professional schools, and required for the efficient pursuit of the other professions, may be serviceable to the community at large; whereas the business proficiency inculcated by the schools of commerce has no such serviceability, being directed singly to a facile command of the ways and means of private gain.[4]

[3] This characterization applies without abatement to the schools of commerce as commonly designed at their foundation and set forth in their public announcements, and to their work in so far as they live up to their professions. At the same time it is to be noted that few of these schools successfully keep their work clear of all entanglement with theoretical discussions that have only a scientific bearing. And it is also quite feasible to organize a "school of commerce" on lines of scientific inquiry, with the avowed purpose of dealing with business enterprise in its various ramifications as subject matter of theoretical investigation; but such is not the avowed aim of the established schools of this class, and such is not the actual character of the work carried on in these schools, except by inadvertence.

[4] It is doubtless within the mark to say that the training given by the American schools of commerce is detrimental to the community's material interests. In America, even in a more pronounced degree than elsewhere, business management centres on financiering and salesmanship; and American commercial schools, even in a more pronounced degree than those of other countries, centre their attention on proficiency in these matters, because these are the matters which the common sense of the American business community knows how to value, and on which it insists as indispensable qualifications in its young men. The besetting infirmity of the American business community, as witness the many and circumstantial disclosures of the "efficiency engineers," and of others who have had occasion to speak of the matter, is a notable indifference to the economical and mechanically efficient use, exploitation and conservation of equipment and resources, coupled with an equally notable want of insight into the technological needs and possibilities of the industries which they control. The typical American businessman watches the industrial process from ambush, with a view to the seizure of any item of value that may be left at loose ends. Business strategy is a strategy of "watchful waiting," at the centre of a web; very alert and adroit, but remarkably incompetent in the way of anything that can properly be called "industrial enterprise."

The concatenation of circumstances that has brought American business enterprise to this inglorious posture, and has virtually engrossed the direction of business affairs in the hands of men endowed with the spiritual and intellectual traits suitable to such prehensile enterprise, can not be gone into here. The fact, however, is patent. It should suffice to call to mind the large fact, as notorious as it is discreditable, that the American business community has, with unexampled

The training that leads up to the several other professions, of course, varies greatly in respect of its draught on scientific information, as well as in the degree of its serviceability to the community; some of the professions, as, e.g., Law, approach very close to the character of business training, both in the unscientific and unscholarly nature of the required training and in their uselessness to the community; while others, as, e.g., Medicine and the various lines of engineering, differ widely from commercial training in both of these respects. With the main exception of Law (and, some would add, of Divinity?) the professional schools train men for work that is of some substantial use to the community at large. This is particularly true of the technological schools. But while the technological schools may be occupied with work that is of substantial use, and while they may draw more or less extensively on the sciences for their materials and even for their methods, they can not, for all that, claim standing in the university on the ground of that disinterested intellectual enterprise which is the university's peculiar domain.

The professional knowledge and skill of physicians, surgeons, dentists, pharmacists, agriculturists, engineers of all kinds, perhaps even of journalists, is of some use to the community at large, at the same time that it may be profitable to the bearers of it. The community has a substantial interest in the adequate training of these men, although it is not that intellectual interest that attaches to science and scholarship. But such is not the case with the training designed to give proficiency in business. No gain comes to the community at large from increasing the business proficiency of any number of its young men. There are already much too many of these businessmen,

---

freedom, had at its disposal the largest and best body of resources that has yet become available to modern industry, in men, materials and geographical situation, and that with these means they have achieved something doubtfully second-rate, as compared with the industrial achievements of other countries less fortunately placed in all material respects.

What the schools of commerce now offer is further specialization along the same line of proficiency, to give increased facility in financiering and salesmanship. This specialization on commerce is like other specialization in that it draws off attention and interest from other lines than those in which the specialization falls; thereby widening the candidate's field of ignorance while it intensifies his effectiveness within his specialty. The effect, as touches the community's interest in the matter, should be an enhancement of the candidate's proficiency in all the futile ways and means of salesmanship and "conspiracy in restraint of trade," together with a heightened incapacity and ignorance bearing on such work as is of material use.

much too astute and proficient in their calling, for the common good. A higher average business efficiency simply raises activity and avidity in business to a higher average pitch of skill and fervour, with very little other material result than a redistribution of ownership; since business is occupied with the competitive acquisition of wealth, not with its production. It is only by a euphemistic metaphor that we are accustomed to speak of the businessmen as producers of goods. Gains due to such efficiency are differential gains only. They are a differential as against other businessmen on the one hand, and as against the rest of the community on the other hand. The work of the College of Commerce, accordingly, is a peculiarly futile line of endeavour for any public institution, in that it serves neither the intellectual advancement nor the material welfare of the community.

The greater the number and the higher the proficiency of the community's businessmen, other things equal, the worse must the rest of the community come off in that game of skilled bargaining and shrewd management by which the businessmen get their gains. Gratuitous or partly gratuitous training for business will presumably increase the number of highly proficient businessmen. As the old-fashioned economists would express it, it will increase the number of "middlemen," of men who "live by their wits." At the same time it should presumably increase the average efficiency of this increased number. The outcome should be that the resulting body of businessmen will be able, between them, to secure a larger proportion of the aggregate wealth of the community; leaving the rest of the community poorer by that much,—except for that (extremely doubtful) amount by which shrewd business management is likely to increase the material wealth-producing capacity of the community. Any such presumed increase of wealth-producing capacity is an incidental concomitant of business traffic, and in the nature of the case it can not equal the aggregate increased gain that goes to the businessmen. At the best the question as to the effect which such an aggregate increased business efficiency will have on the community's material welfare is a question of how large the net loss will be; that it will entail a net loss on the community at large is in fact not an open question.

A college of commerce is designed to serve an emulative purpose only—individual gain regardless of, or at the cost of, the community at large—and it is, therefore, peculiarly incompatible with the collective cultural purpose of the university. It belongs in the corporation of learning no more than a department of athletics.[5] Both alike give training that is of no use to the community,—except, perhaps, as a sentimental excitement. Neither business proficiency nor proficiency in athletic contests need be decried, of course. They have their value, to the businessmen and to the athletes, respectively, chiefly as a means of livelihood at the cost of the rest of the community, and it is to be presumed that they are worth while to those who go in for that sort of thing. Both alike are related to the legitimate ends of the university as a drain on its resources and an impairment of its scholarly animus. As related to the ostensible purposes of a university, therefore, the support and conduct of such schools at the expense of the universities is to be construed as a breach of trust.

[5] Latterly, it appears, the training given by the athletic establishments attached to the universities is also coming to have a value as vocational training; in that the men so trained and vouched for by these establishments are finding lucrative employment as instructors, coaches, masseurs, etc., engaged in similar athletic traffic in various schools, public or private. So also, and for the same reason, they are found eligible as "muscular Christian" secretaries in charge of chapters of the Y.M.C.A. and the like quasi-devout clubs and gilds. Indeed in all but the name, the athletic establishments are taking on the character of "schools" or "divisions" included under the collective academic administration, very much after the fashion of a "School of Education" or a "School of Journalism"; and they are in effect "graduating" students in Athletics, with due, though hitherto unofficial, certification of proficiency. So also, latterly, one meets with proposals, made in good faith, among official academic men to allow due "academic credit" for training in athletics and let it count toward graduation. By indirection and subreption, of course, much of the training given in athletics already does so count.

3

Why Is Economics Not an Evolutionary Science?*

This essay, reproduced in its entirety, is a kind of touchstone by which many of Veblen's basic ideas may be measured and tested. Let the reader ask himself how well they fare now, more than sixty years after their author set them forth. It will perhaps appear here and there that Veblen is flailing a straw man. Many of his enemies have been routed. If so, this is at least in some small part a tribute to the cogency of his arguments. Although there may be less descriptive taxonomy today, enough remains to provoke the critic. While classical economics has declined, "the traditional wisdom" (as John K. Galbraith likes to call it) still has many champions. They have not yet disembarrassed themselves fully of the hedonistic theory or of the tendency to impute a higher purpose to history or of the inclination to isolate economic activity from the total context of human culture. "Impersonal sequence" and "cumulative causation" remain the best vantage point from which to view social, economic, and political behavior. Nowadays, this cannot be repeated too often. Few men have said it with greater subtlety, skill, clarity, and wit than Thorstein Veblen—and nowhere more so than in "Why Is Economics Not an Evolutionary Science?"

M. G. de Lapouge recently said, "Anthropology is destined to revolutionise the political and the social sciences as radically as bacteriology has revolutionised the science of medicine." In so far as he speaks of economics, the eminent anthropologist is not alone in his conviction that the science stands in need of rehabilitation. His words convey a

* From *The Quarterly Journal of Economics,* XII (July, 1898), 56–81.

rebuke and an admonition, and in both respects he speaks the sense of many scientists in his own and related lines of inquiry. It may be taken as the consensus of those men who are doing the serious work of modern anthropology, ethnology, and psychology, as well as of those in the biological sciences proper, that economics is helplessly behind the times, and unable to handle its subject-matter in a way to entitle it to standing as a modern science. The other political and social sciences come in for their share of this obloquy, and perhaps on equally cogent grounds. Nor are the economists themselves buoyantly indifferent to the rebuke. Probably no economist to-day has either the hardihood or the inclination to say that the science has now reached a definitive formulation, either in the detail of results or as regards the fundamental features of theory. The nearest recent approach to such a position on the part of an economist of accredited standing is perhaps to be found in Professor Marshall's Cambridge address of a year and a half ago. But these utterances are so far from the jaunty confidence shown by the classical economists of half a century ago that what most forcibly strikes the reader of Professor Marshall's address is the exceeding modesty and the uncalled-for humility of the spokesman for the "old generation." With the economists who are most attentively looked to for guidance, uncertainty as to the definitive value of what has been and is being done, and as to what we may, with effect, take to next, is so common as to suggest that indecision is a meritorious work. Even the Historical School, who made their innovation with so much home-grown applause some time back, have been unable to settle down contentedly to the pace which they set themselves.

The men of the sciences that are proud to own themselves "modern" find fault with the economists for being still content to occupy themselves with repairing a structure and doctrines and maxims resting on natural rights, utilitarianism, and administrative expediency. This aspersion is not altogether merited, but is near enough to the mark to carry a sting. These modern sciences are evolutionary sciences, and their adepts contemplate that characteristic of their work with some complacency. Economics is not an evolutionary science—by the confession of its spokesmen; and the economists turn their eyes with something of envy and some sense of baffled emulation to these rivals that make broad their phylacteries with the legend, "Up to date."

Precisely wherein the social and political sciences, including economics, fall short of being evolutionary sciences, is not so plain. At least, it has not been satisfactorily pointed out by their critics. Their successful rivals in this matter—the sciences that deal with human nature among the rest—claim as their substantial distinction that they are realistic: they deal with facts. But economics, too, is realistic in this sense: it deals with facts, often in the most painstaking way, and latterly with an increasingly strenuous insistence on the sole efficacy of data. But this "realism" does not make economics an evolutionary science. The insistence on data could scarcely be carried to a higher pitch than it was carried by the first generation of the Historical School; and yet no economics is farther from being an evolutionary science than the received economics of the Historical School. The whole broad range of erudition and research that engaged the energies of that school commonly falls short of being science, in that, when consistent, they have contented themselves with an enumeration of data and a narrative account of industrial development, and have not presumed to offer a theory of anything or to elaborate their results into a consistent body of knowledge.

Any evolutionary science, on the other hand, is a close-knit body of theory. It is a theory of a process, of an unfolding sequence. But here, again, economics seems to meet the test in a fair measure, without satisfying its critics that its credentials are good. It must be admitted, e.g., that J. S. Mill's doctrines of production, distribution, and exchange, are a theory of certain economic processes, and that he deals in a consistent and effective fashion with the sequences of fact that make up his subject-matter. So, also, Cairnes's discussion of normal value, of the rate of wages, and of international trade, are excellent instances of a theoretical handling of economic processes of sequence and the orderly unfolding development of fact. But an attempt to cite Mill and Cairnes as exponents of an evolutionary economics will produce no better effect than perplexity, and not a great deal of that. Very much of monetary theory might be cited to the same purpose and with the like effect. Something similar is true even of late writers who have avowed some penchant for the evolutionary point of view; as, e.g., Professor Hadley,—to cite a work of unquestioned merit and unusual reach. Measurably, he keeps the word of promise to the ear; but any one who may cite his *Economics* as having brought political economy into line as an evolutionary science will convince neither himself nor his interlocutor. Something to the like effect may fairly be said of the published work of that later English strain of economists represented by Professors Cunningham and Ashley, and Mr. Cannan, to name but a few of the more eminent figures in the group.

Of the achievements of the classical economists, recent and living, the science may justly be proud; but they fall short of the evolutionist's standard of adequacy, not in failing to offer a theory of a process or of a developmental relation, but through conceiving their theory in terms alien to the evolutionist's habits of thought. The difference between the evolutionary and the pre-evolutionary sciences lies not in the insistence on facts. There was a great and fruitful activity in the natural sciences in collecting and collating facts before these sciences took on the character which marks them as evolutionary. Nor does the difference lie in the absence of efforts to formulate and explain schemes of process, sequence, growth, and development in the pre-evolutionary days. Efforts of this kind abounded, in number and diversity; and many schemes of development, of great subtlety and beauty, gained a vogue both as theories of organic and inorganic development and as schemes of the life history of nations and societies. It will not even hold true that our elders overlooked the presence of cause and effect in formulating their theories and reducing their data to a body of knowledge. But the terms which were accepted as the definitive terms of knowledge were in some degree different in the early days from what they are now. The terms of thought in which the investigators of some two or three generations back definitively formulated their knowledge of facts, in their last analyses, were different in kind from the terms in which the modern evolutionist is content to formulate his results. The analysis does not run back to the same ground, or appeal to the same standard of finality or adequacy, in the one case as in the other.

The difference is a difference of spiritual attitude or point of view in the two contrasted generations of scientists. To put the matter in other words, it is a difference in the basis of valuation of the facts for the scientific purpose, or in the interest from which the facts are appreciated. With the earlier as with the later generation the basis of valuation of the facts handled is, in matters of detail, the causal relation which is apprehended to subsist between them. This is true to the greatest extent for the natural sciences. But in their handling of the more comprehensive schemes of sequence and relation—in their definitive formulation of the results—the two generations differ. The modern scientist is unwilling to depart from the test of causal relation or quantitative sequence. When he asks the question, Why? he insists on an answer in terms of cause and effect. He wants to reduce his solution of all problems to terms of the conservation of energy or the persistence of quantity. This is his last recourse. And this last recourse has in our time been made available for the handling of schemes of development and theories of a comprehensive process by the notion of a cumulative causation. The great deserts of the evolutionist leaders—if they have great deserts as leaders—lie, on the one hand, in their refusal to go back of the colorless sequence of phenomena and seek higher ground for their ultimate syntheses, and, on the other hand, in their having shown how this colorless impersonal sequence of cause and effect can be made use of for theory proper, by virtue of its cumulative character.

For the earlier natural scientists, as for the classical economists, this ground of cause and effect is not definitive. Their sense of truth and substantiality is not satisfied with a formulation of mechanical sequence. The ultimate term in their systematisation of knowledge is a "natural law." This natural law is felt to exercise some sort of a coercive surveillance over the sequence of events, and to give a spiritual stability and consistence to the causal relation at any given juncture. To meet the high classical requirement, a sequence—and a developmental process especially—must be apprehended in terms of a consistent propensity tending to some spiritually legitimate end. When facts and events have been reduced to these terms of fundamental truth and have been made to square with the requirements of definitive normality, the investigator rests his case. Any causal sequence which is apprehended to traverse the imputed propensity in events is a "disturbing factor." Logical congruity with the apprehended propensity is, in this view, adequate ground of procedure in building up a scheme of knowledge or of development. The objective point of the efforts of the scientists working under the guidance of this classical tradition, is to formulate knowledge in terms of aboslute truth; and this absolute truth is a spiritual fact. It means a coincidence of facts with the deliverances of an enlightened and deliberate common sense.

The development and the attenuation of this preconception of normality or of a propensity in events might be traced in detail from primitive animism down through the elaborate discipline of faith and metaphysics, overruling Providence, order of nature, natural rights, natural law, underlying principles. But all that may be necessary here is to point out that, by descent and by psychological content, this constraining normality is of a spiritual kind. It is for the scientific purpose an imputation of spiritual coherence to the facts dealt with. The question of interest is how this preconception of normality has fared at the hands of modern science, and how it has come to be superseded in the intellectual primacy by the latter-day preconception of a non-spiritual sequence. This question is of interest because its answer may throw light on the question as to what chance there is for the indefinite persistence of this archaic habit of thought in the methods of economic science.

Under primitive conditions, men stand in immediate personal contact with the material facts of the environment; and the force and discretion of the individual in shaping the facts of the environment count obviously, and to all appearance solely, in working out the conditions of life. There is little of impersonal or mechanical sequence visible to primitive men in their every-day life; and what there is of this kind in the processes of brute nature about them is in large part inexplicable and passes for inscrutable. It is accepted as malignant or beneficent, and is construed in the terms of personality that are familiar to all men at first hand,—the terms known to all men by first-hand knowledge of their own acts. The inscrutable movements of the seasons and of the natural forces are apprehended as actions guided by discretion, will power, or propensity looking to an end, much as human actions are. The processes of inanimate nature are agencies whose habits of life are to be learned, and who are to be coerced, outwitted, circumvented, and turned to account, much as the beasts are. At the same time the community is small, and the human contact of the individual is not wide. Neither the industrial life nor the non-industrial social life forces upon men's attention the ruthless impersonal sweep of events that no man can withstand or deflect, such as becomes visible in the more complex and comprehensive life process of the larger community of a later day. There is nothing decisive to hinder men's knowledge of facts and events being formulated in terms of personality—in terms of habit and propensity and will power.

As time goes on and as the situation departs from this archaic character,—where it does depart from it,—the circumstances which condition men's systematisation of facts change in such a way as to throw the impersonal character of the sequence of events more and more into the foreground. The penalties for failure to apprehend facts in dispassionate terms fall surer and swifter. The sweep of events is forced home more consistently on men's minds. The guiding hand of a spiritual agency or a propensity in events becomes less readily traceable as men's knowledge of things grows ampler and more searching. In modern times, and particularly in the industrial countries, this coercive guidance of men's habits of thought in the realstic direction has been especially pronounced; and the effect shows itself in a somewhat reluctant but cumulative departure from the arhcaic point of view. The departure is most visible and has gone farthest in those homely branches of knowledge that have to do immediately with modern mechanical processes, such as engineering designs and technological contrivances generally. Of the sciences, those have wandered farthest on this way (of integration or disintegration, according as one may choose to view it) that have to do with mechanical sequence and process; and those have best and longest retained the archaic point of view intact which—like the moral, social, or spiritual sciences—have to do with process and sequence that is less tangible, less traceable by the use of the senses, and that therefore less immediately forces upon the attention the phenomenon of sequence as contrasted with that of propensity.

There is no abrupt transition from the pre-evolutionary to the post-evolutionary standpoint. Even in those natural sciences which deal with the processes of life and the evolutionary sequence of events the concept of dispassionate cumulative causation has often and effectively been helped out by the notion that there is in all this some sort of a meliorative trend that exercises a constraining guidance over the course of causes and effects. The faith in this meliorative trend as a concept useful to the science has gradually weakened, and it has repeatedly been disavowed; but it can scarcely be said to have yet disappeared from the field.

The process of change in the point of view, or in the terms of definitive formulation of knowledge, is a gradual one; and all the sciences have shared, though in an unequal degree, in the change that is going forward. Economics is not an exception to the rule, but it still shows too many reminiscences of the "natural" and the "normal," of "verities" and "tendencies," of "controlling principles" and "disturbing causes" to be classed as an evolutionary science. This history of the science shows a long and devious course of disintegrating animism,—from the days of the scholastic writers, who discussed usury from the point of view of its relation to the divine suzerainty, to the Physiocrats, who rested their case on an "*ordre naturel*" and a "*loi naturelle*" that decides what is substantially true and, in a general way, guides the course of events by the constraint of logical congruence. There has been something of a change from Adam Smith, whose recourse in perplexity was to the guidance of "an unseen hand," to Mill and Cairnes, who formulated the laws of "natural" wages and "normal" value, and the former of whom was so well content with his work as to say, "Happily, there is nothing in the laws of Value which remains for the present or any future writer to clear up: the theory of the subject is complete." But the difference between the earlier and the later point of view is a difference of degree rather than of kind.

The standpoint of the classical economists, in their higher or definitive syntheses and generalisations, may not inaptly be called the standpoint of ceremonial adequacy. The ultimate laws and principles which they formulated were laws of the normal or the natural, according to a preconception regarding the ends to which, in the nature of things, all things tend. In effect, this preconception imputes to things a tendency to work out what the instructed common sense of the time accepts as the adequate or worthy end of human effort. It is a projection of the accepted ideal of conduct. This ideal of conduct is made to serve as a canon of truth, to the extent that the investigator contents himself with an appeal to its legitimation for premises that run back of the facts with which he is immediately dealing, for the "controlling principles" that are conceived intangibly to underlie the process discussed, and for the "tendencies" that run beyond the situation as it lies before him. As instances of the use of this ceremonial canon of knowledge may be cited the "conjectural history" that plays so large a part in the classical treatment of economic institutions, such as the normalized accounts of the beginnings of barter in the transactions of the putative hunter, fisherman, and boat-builder, or the man with the plane and the two planks, or the two men with the basket of apples and the basket of nuts. Of a similar import is the characterisation of money as "the great wheel of circulation" or as "the medium of exchange." Money is here discussed in terms of the end which, "in the normal case," it should work out according to the given writer's ideal of economic life, rather than in terms of causal relation.

With later writers especially, this terminology is no doubt to be commonly taken as a convenient use of metaphor, in which the concept of normality and propensity to an end has reached an extreme attenuation. But it is precisely in this use of figurative terms for the formulation of theory that the classical normality still lives its attenuated life in modern economics; and it is this facile recourse to inscrutable figures of speech as the ultimate terms of theory that has saved the economists from being dragooned into the ranks of modern science. The metaphors are effective, both in their homilectical use and as a labor-saving device,—more effective than their user designs them to be. By their use the theorist is enabled serenely to enjoin himself from following out an elusive train of causal sequence. He is also enabled, without misgivings, to construct a theory of such an institution as money or wages or land-ownership without descending to a consideration of the living items concerned, except for convenient corroboration of his normalised scheme of symptoms. By this method the theory of an institution or a phase of life may be stated in conventionalised terms of the apparatus whereby life is carried on, the apparatus being invested with a tendency to an equilibrium at the normal, and the theory being a formulation of the conditions under which this putative equilibrium supervenes. In this way we have come into the usufruct of a cost-of-production theory of value which is pungently reminiscent of the time when Nature abhorred a vacuum. The ways and means and the mechanical structure of industry are formulated in a conventionalised nomenclature, and the observed motions of this mechanical apparatus are then reduced to a normalised scheme of relations. The scheme so arrived at is spiritually binding on the behavior of the phenomena contemplated. With this normalised scheme as a guide, the permutations of a given segment of the apparatus are worked out according to the values assigned the several items and features comprised in the calculation; and a ceremonially consistent formula is constructed to cover that much of the industrial field. This is the deductive method. The formula is then tested by comparison with observed permutations, by the polariscopic use of the "normal case"; and the results arrived at are thus authenticated by induction. Features of the process that do not lend themselves to interpretation in the terms of the formula are abnormal cases and are due to disturbing causes. In all this the agencies or forces causally at work in the economic life process are neatly avoided. The outcome of the method, at its best, is a body of logically consistent propositions concerning the normal relations of things—a system of economic taxonomy. At its worst, it is a body of maxims for the conduct of business and a polemical discussion of disputed points of policy.

In all this, economic science is living over again in its turn the experiences which the natural sciences passed through some time back. In the natural sciences the work of the taxonomist was and continues to be of great value, but the scientists grew restless under the régime of symmetry and system-making. They took to asking why, and so shifted their inquiries from the structure of the coral reefs to the structure and habits of life of the polyp that lives in and by them. In the science of plants, systematic botany has not ceased to be of service; but the stress of investigation and discussion among the botanists today falls on the biological value of any given feature of structure, function, or tissue rather than on its taxonomic bearing. All the talk about cytoplasm, centrosomes, and karyokinetic process, means that the inquiry now looks consistently to the life process, and aims to explain it in terms of cumulative causation.

What may be done in economic science of the taxonomic kind is shown at its best in Cairnes's work, where the method is well conceived and the results effectively formulated and applied. Cairnes handles the theory of the normal case in economic life with a master hand. In his discussion the metaphysics of propensity and tendencies no longer avowedly rules the formulation of theory, nor is the inscrutable meliorative trend of a harmony of interests confidently appealed to as an engine of definitive use in giving legitimacy to the economic situation at a given time. There is less of an exercise of faith in Cairnes's economic discussions than in those of the writers that went before him. The definitive terms of the formulation are still the terms of normality and natural law, but the metaphysics underlying this appeal to normality is so far removed from the ancient ground of the beneficent "order of nature" as to have become at least nominally impersonal and to proceed without a constant regard to the humanitarian bearing of the "tendencies" which it formulates. The metaphysics has been attenuated to something approaching in colorlessness the naturalist's conception of natural law. It is a natural law which, in the guise of "controlling principles," exercises a constraining surveillance over the trend of things; but it is no longer conceived to exercise its constraint in the interest of certain ulterior human purposes. The element of beneficence has been well-nigh eliminated, and the system is formulated in terms of the system itself.

Economics as it left Cairnes's hand, so far as his theoretical work is concerned, comes near being taxonomy for taxonomy's sake.

No equally capable writer has come as near making economics the ideal "dismal" science as Cairnes in his discussion of pure theory. In the days of the early classical writers economics had a vital interest for the laymen of the time, because it formulated the common sense metaphysics of the time in its application to a department of human life. But in the hands of the later classical writers the science lost much of its charm in this regard. It was no longer a definition and authentication of the deliverances of current common sense as to what ought to come to pass; and it, therefore, in large measure lost the support of the people out of doors, who were unable to take an interest in what did not concern them; and it was also out of touch with that realistic or evolutionary habit of mind which got under way about the middle of the century in the natural sciences. It was neither vitally metaphysical nor matter-of-fact, and it found comfort with very few outside of its own ranks. Only for those who by the fortunate accident of birth or education have been able to conserve the taxonomic animus has the science during the last third of a century continued to be of absorbing interest. The result has been that from the time when the taxonomic structure stood forth as a completed whole in its symmetry and stability the economists themselves, beginning with Cairnes, have been growing restive under its discipline of stability, and have made many efforts, more or less sustained, to galvanise it into movement. At the hands of the writers of the classical line these excursions have chiefly aimed at a more complete and comprehensive taxonomic scheme of permutations; while the historical departure threw away the taxonomic ideal without getting rid of the preconceptions on which it is based; and the later Austrian group struck out on a theory of process, but presently came to a full stop because the process about which they busied themselves was not, in their apprehension of it, a cumulative or unfolding sequence.

But what does all this signify? If we are getting restless under the taxonomy of a monocotyledonous wage doctrine and a cryptogamic theory of interest, with involute, loculicidal, tomentous and moniliform variants, what is the cytoplasm, centrosome, or karyokinetic process to which we may turn, and in which we may find surcease from the metaphysics of normality and controlling principles? What are we going to do about it? The question is rather, What are we doing about it? There is the economic life process still in great measure awaiting theoretical formulation. The active material in which the economic process goes on is the human material of the industrial community. For the purpose of economic science the process of cumulative change that is to be accounted for is the sequence of change in the methods of doing things,—the methods of dealing with the material means of life.

What has been done in the way of inquiry into this economic life process? The ways and means of turning material objects and circumstances to account lie before the investigator at any given point of time in the form of mechanical contrivances and arrangements for compassing certain mechanical ends. It has therefore been easy to accept these ways and means as items of inert matter having a given mechanical structure and thereby serving the material ends of man. As such, they have been scheduled and graded by the economists under the head of capital, this capital being conceived as a mass of material objects serviceable for human use. This is well enough for the purposes of taxonomy; but it is not an effective method of conceiving the matter for the purpose of a theory of the developmental process. For the latter purpose, when taken as items in a process of cumulative change or as items in the scheme of life, these productive goods are facts of human knowledge, skill, and predilection; that is to say, they are, substantially, prevalent habits of thought, and it is as such that they enter into the process of industrial development. The physical properties of the materials accessible to man are constants: it is the human agent that changes,—his insight and his appreciation of what these things can be used for is what develops. The accumulation of goods already on hand conditions his handling and utilisation of the materials offered, but even on this side—the "limitation of industry by capital"—the limitation imposed is on what men can do and on the methods of doing it. The changes that take place in the mechanical contrivances are an expression of changes in the human factor. Changes in the material facts breed further change only through the human factor. It is in the human material that the continuity of development is to be looked for; and it is here, therefore, that the motor forces of the process of economic development must be studied if they are to be studied in action at all. Economic action must be the subject-matter of the science if the science is to fall into line as an evolutionary science.

Nothing new has been said in all this. But the fact is all the more significant for being a familiar fact. It is a fact recognised by common consent throughout much of the later economic discussion, and this current recognition of the fact is a long step towards centering discussion and inquiry upon it. If economics is to follow the lead or the analogy of the other sciences that have to do with a life process, the way is plain so far as regards the general direction in which the move will be made.

The economists of the classical trend have made no serious attempt to depart from the standpoint of taxonomy and make their science a genetic account of the economic life process. As has just been said, much the same is true for the Historical School. The latter have attempted an account of developmental sequence, but they have followed the lines of pre-Darwinian speculations on development rather than lines which modern science would recognise as evolutionary. They have given a narrative survey of phenomena, not a genetic account of an unfolding process. In this work they have, no doubt, achieved results of permanent value; but the results achieved are scarcely to be classed as economic theory. On the other hand, the Austrians and their precursors and their co-adjutors in the value discussion have taken up a detached portion of economic theory, and have inquired with great nicety into the process by which the phenomena within their limited field are worked out. The entire discussion of marginal utility and subjective value as the outcome of a valuation process must be taken as a genetic study of this range of facts. But here, again, nothing further has come of the inquiry, so far as regards a rehabilitation of economic theory as a whole. Accepting Menger as their spokesman on this head, it must be said that the Austrians have on the whole showed themselves unable to break with the classical tradition that economics is a taxonomic science.

The reason for the Austrian failure seems to lie in a faulty conception of human nature,—faulty for the present purpose, however adequate it may be for any other. In all the received formulations of economic theory, whether at the hands of English economists or those of the Continent, the human material with which the inquiry is concerned is conceived in hedonistic terms; that is to say, in terms of a passive and substantially inert and immutably given human nature. The psychological and anthropological preconceptions of the economists have been those which were accepted by the psychological and social sciences some generations ago. The hedonistic conception of man is that of a lightning calculator of pleasures and pains, who oscillates like a homogeneous globule of desire of happiness under the impulse of stimuli that shift him about the area, but leave him intact. He has neither antecedent nor consequent. He is an isolated, definitive human datum, in stable equilibrium except for the buffets of the impinging forces that displace him in one direction or another. Self-imposed in elemental space, he spins symmetrically about his own spiritual axis until the parallelogram of forces bears down upon him, whereupon he follows the line of the resultant. When the force of the impact is spent, he comes to rest, a self-contained globule of desire as before. Spiritually, the hedonistic man is not a prime mover. He is not the seat of a process of living, except in the sense that he is subject to a series of permutations enforced upon him by circumstances external and alien to him.

The later psychology, reënforced by modern anthropological research, gives a different conception of human nature. According to this conception, it is the characteristic of man to do something, not simply to suffer pleasures and pains through the impact of suitable forces. He is not simply a bundle of desires that are to be saturated by being placed in the path of the forces of the environment, but rather a coherent structure of propensities and habits which seeks realisation and expression in an unfolding activity. According to this view, human activity, and economic activity among the rest, is not apprehended as something incidental to the process of saturating given desires. The activity is itself the substantial fact of the process, and the desires under whose guidance the action takes place are circumstances of temperament which determine the specific direction in which the activity will unfold itself in the given case. These circumstances of temperament are ultimate and definitive for the individual who acts under them, so far as regards his attitude as agent in the particular action in which he is engaged. But, in the view of the science, they are elements of the existing frame of mind of the agent, and are the outcome of his antecedents and his life up to the point at which he stands. They are the products of his hereditary traits and his past experience, cumulatively wrought out under a given body of traditions, conventionalities, and material circumstances; and they afford the point of departure for the next step in the process. The economic life history of the individual is a cumulative process of adaptation of means to ends that cumulatively change as the process goes on, both the agent and his environment being at any point the outcome of the last process. His methods of life to-day are enforced upon him by his habits of life carried over from yesterday and by the circumstances left as the mechanical residue of the life of yesterday.

What is true of the individual in this respect is true of the group in which he lives. All economic change is a change in the economic community,—a change in the community's methods of turning material things to account. The change is always in the last resort a change in habits of thought. This is true even of changes in the mechanical processes of industry. A given contrivance for effecting certain material ends becomes a circumstance which affects the further growth of habits of thought—habitual methods of procedure—and so becomes a point of departure for further development of the methods of compassing the ends sought and for the further variation of ends that are sought to be compassed. In all this flux there is no definitively adequate method of life and no definitive or absolutely worthy end of action, so far as concerns the science which sets out to formulate a theory of the process of economic life. What remains as a hard and fast residue is the fact of activity directed to an objective end. Economic action is teleological, in the sense that men always and everywhere seek to do something. What, in specific detail, they seek, is not to be answered except by a scrutiny of the details of their activity; but, so long as we have to do with their life as members of the economic community, there remains the generic fact that their life is an unfolding activity of a teleological kind.

It may or may not be a teleological process in the sense that it tends or should tend to any end that is conceived to be worthy or adequate by the inquirer or by the consensus of inquirers. Whether it is or is not, is a question with which the present inquiry is not concerned; and it is also a question of which an evolutionary economics need take no account. The question of a tendency in events can evidently not come up except on the ground of some preconception or prepossession on the part of the person looking for the tendency. In order to search for a tendency, we must be possessed of some notion of a definitive end to be sought, or some notion as to what is the legitimate trend of events. The notion of a legitimate trend in a course of events is an extra-evolutionary preconception, and lies outside the scope of an inquiry into the causal sequence in any process.

The evolutionary point of view, therefore, leaves no place for a formulation of natural laws in terms of definitive normality, whether in economics or in any other branch of inquiry. Neither does it leave room for that other question of normality, What should be the end of the developmental process under discussion?

The economic life history of any community is its life history in so far as it is shaped by men's interest in the material means of life. This economic interest has counted for much in shaping the cultural growth of all communities. Primarily and most obviously, it has guided the formation, the cumulative growth, of that range of conventionalities and methods of life that are currently recognized as economic institutions; but the same interest has also pervaded the community's life and its cultural growth at points where the resulting structural features are not chiefly and most immediately of an economic bearing. The economic interest goes with men through life, and it goes with the race throughout its process of cultural development. It affects the cultural structure at all points, so that all institutions may be said to be in some measure economic institutions. This is necessarily the case, since the base of action—the point of departure—at any step in the process is the entire organic complex of habits of thought that have been shaped by the past process. The economic interest does not act in isolation, for it is but one of several vaguely isolable interests on which the complex of teleological activity carried out by the individual proceeds. The individual is but a single agent in each case; and he enters into each successive action as a whole, although the specific end sought in a given action may be sought avowedly on the basis of a particular interest; as, e.g., the economic, æsthetic, sexual, humanitarian, devotional interests. Since each of these passably isolable interests is a propensity of the organic agent man, with his complex of habits of thought, the expression of each is affected by habits of life formed under the guidance of all the rest. There is, therefore, no neatly isolable range of cultural phenomena that can be rigorously set apart under the head of economic institutions, although a category of "economic institutions" may be of service as a convenient caption, comprising those institutions in which the economic interest most immediately and consistently finds expression, and which most immediately and with the least limitation are of an economic bearing.

From what has been said it appears that an evolutionary economics must be the theory of a process of cultural growth as determined by the economic interest, a theory of a cumulative sequence of economic institutions stated in terms of the process itself. Except for the want of space to do here what should be done in some detail if it is done at all, many efforts by the later economists in this direction might be cited to show the trend of economic discussion in this direction. There is not a little evidence to this effect, and much of the work done must be rated as effective work for this purpose. Much of the work of the Historical School, for instance, and that of its later exponents especially, is too noteworthy to be passed over in silence, even with all due regard to the limitations of space.

We are now ready to return to the question why economics is not an evolutionary science. It is necessarily the aim of such an economics to trace the cumulative working-out of the economic interest in the cultural sequence. It must be a theory of the economic life process of the race or the community. The economists have accepted the hedonistic preconceptions concerning human nature and human action, and the conception of the economic interest which a hedonistic psychology gives does not afford material for a theory of the development of human nature. Under hedonism the economic interest is not conceived in terms of action. It is therefore not readily apprehended or appreciated in terms of a cumulative growth of habits of thought, and does not provoke, even if it did lend itself to, treatment by the evolutionary method. At the same time the anthropological preconceptions current in that common-sense apprehension of human nature to which economists have habitually turned has not enforced the formulation of human nature in terms of a cumulative growth of habits of life. These received anthropological preconceptions are such as have made possible the normalized conjectural accounts of primitive barter with which all economic readers are familiar, and the no less normalized conventional derivation of landed property and its rent, or the sociologico-philosophical discussions of the "function" of this or that class in the life of society or of the nation.

The premises and the point of view required for an evolutionary economics have been wanting. The economists have not had the materials for such a science ready to their hand, and the provocation to strike out in such a direction has been absent. Even if it has been possible at any time to turn to the evolutionary line of speculation in economics, the possibility of a departure is not enough to bring it about. So long as the habitual view taken of a given range of facts is of the taxonomic kind and the material lends itself to treatment by that method, the taxonomic method is the easiest, gives the most gratifying immediate results, and best fits into the accepted body of knowledge of the range of facts in question. This has been the situation in economics. The other sciences of its group have likewise been a body of taxonomic discipline, and departures from the accredited method have lain under the odium of being meretricious innovations. The well-worn paths are easy to follow and lead into good company. Advance along them visibly furthers the accredited work which the science has in hand. Divergence from the paths means tentative work, which is necessarily slow and fragmentary and of uncertain value.

It is only when the methods of the science and the syntheses resulting from their use come to be out of line with habits of thought that prevail in other matters that the scientist grows restive under the guidance of the received methods and standpoints, and seeks a way out. Like other men, the economist is an individual with but one intelligence. He is a creature of habits and propensities given through the antecedents, hereditary and cultural, of which he is an outcome; and the habits of thought formed in any one line of experience affect his thinking in any other. Methods of observation and of handling facts that are familiar through habitual use in the general range of knowledge, gradually assert themselves in any given special range of knowledge. They may be accepted slowly and with reluctance where their acceptance involves innovation; but, if they have the continued backing of the general body of experience, it is only a question of time when they shall come into dominance in the special field. The intellectual attitude and the method of correlation enforced upon us in the apprehension and assimilation of facts in the more elementary ranges of knowledge that have to do with brute facts assert themselves also when the attention is directed to those phenomena of the life process with which economics has to do; and the range of facts which are habitually handled by other methods than that in traditional vogue in economics has now become so large and so insistently present at every turn that we are left restless, if the new body of facts cannot be handled according to the method of mental procedure which is in this way becoming habitual.

In the general body of knowledge in modern times the facts are apprehended in terms of causal sequence. This is especially true of that knowledge of brute facts which is shaped by the exigencies of the modern mechanical industry. To men thoroughly imbued with this matter-of-fact habit of mind the laws and theorems of economics, and of the other sciences that treat of the normal course of things, have a character of "unreality" and futility that bars out any serious interest in their discussion. The laws and theorems are "unreal" to them because they are not to be apprehended in the terms which these men make use of in handling the facts with which they are per force habitually occupied. The same matter-of-fact spiritual attitude and mode of procedure have now made their way well up into the higher levels of scientific knowledge, even in the sciences which deal in a more elementary way with the same human material that makes the subject-matter of economics, and the economists themselves are beginning to feel the unreality of their theorems about "normal" cases. Provided the practical exigencics of modern industrial life continue of the same character as they now are, and so continue to enforce the impersonal method of knowledge, it is only a question of time when that (substantially animistic) habit of mind which proceeds on the notion of a definitive normality shall be displaced in the field of economic inquiry by that (substantially materialistic) habit of mind which seeks a comprehension of facts in terms of a cumulative sequence.

The later method of apprehending and assimilating facts and handling them for the purposes of knowledge may be better or worse, more or less worthy or adequate, than the earlier; it may be of greater or less ceremonial or æsthetic effect; we may be moved to regret the incursion of underbred habits of thought into the scholar's domain. But all that is beside the present point. Under the stress of modern technological exigencies, men's everyday habits of thought are falling into the lines that in the sciences constitute the evolutionary method; and knowledge which proceeds on a higher, more archaic plane is becoming alien and meaningless to them. The social and political sciences must follow the drift, for they are already caught in it.

4

The Socialist Economics of Karl Marx and His Followers*

The following admirable exposition of Marx and Marxism originally appeared as Part I of a two-part analysis published in 1906 and 1907 in The Quarterly Journal of Economics. *The articles were themselves based upon a series of lectures Veblen had delivered at Harvard University a short time before. Every page should make it clear beyond cavil that Veblen did not and could not regard himself as a Marxist. The non-Marxist and anti-Marxist point of view he implicitly expressed almost everywhere else is made explicit and unambiguous in this material.*

Veblen was superbly equipped for the critical task he set himself in the Harvard lectures. Few men could have traced the Marxist derivation and the Marxist intention as well as he. Indeed, although the literature has waxed and swollen, no one has to date gone more directly and thoroughly to the heart of the matter. We have already alluded in the Introduction to the principal criticisms made by Veblen. One should perhaps add the weightiest of these: "The facts are not bearing it [Marxist theory] out on certain critical points, such as the doctrine of increasing misery; and the Hegelian philosophical postulates, without which the Marxism of Marx is groundless, are for the most part forgotten by the dogmatists of to-day." Veblen traces Marxist doctrine with a sure hand; as such he is a sociologist of knowledge. He does not commit the cardinal sin of exposing origins to show that ideas which grew out of them are invalid. On the contrary, his standards are empirical and logical. Marx made inaccurate predictions because his system was faulty. Veblen rejected

* From *The Quarterly Journal of Economics,* XX (August, 1906), 409–30.

Marxism not by a demonstration of some of its connections with utilitarian and Hegelian philosophy, but on independent scientific grounds. He pierced the aura of religious devotion that even then surrounded this body of thought. It might not have occurred to him that Marxism would become a new world religion, but then, there are limits to any man's prescience.

The system of doctrines worked out by Marx is characterised by a certain boldness of conception and a great logical consistency. Taken in detail, the constituent elements of the system are neither novel nor iconoclastic, nor does Marx at any point claim to have discovered previously hidden facts or to have invented recondite formulations of facts already known; but the system as a whole has an air of originality and initiative such as is rarely met with among the sciences that deal with any phase of human culture. How much of this distinctive character the Marxian system owes to the personal traits of its creator is not easy to say, but what marks it off from all other systems of economic theory is not a matter of personal idiosyncrasy. It differs characteristically from all systems of theory that had preceded it, both in its premises and in its aims. The (hostile) critics of Marx have not sufficiently appreciated the radical character of his departure in both of these respects, and have, therefore, commonly lost themselves in a tangled scrutiny of supposedly abstruse details; whereas those writers who have been in sympathy with his teachings have too commonly been disciples bent on exegesis and on confirming their fellow-disciples in the faith.

Except as a whole and except in the light of its postulates and aims, the Marxian system is not only not tenable, but it is not even intelligible. A discussion of a given isolated feature of the system (such as the theory of value) from the point of view of classical economics (such as that offered by Böhm-Bawerk) is as futile as a discussion of solids in terms of two dimensions.

Neither as regards his postulates and preconceptions nor as regards the aim of his inquiry is Marx's position an altogether single-minded one. In neither respect does his position come of a single line of antecedents. He is of no single school of philosophy, nor are his ideals those of any single group of speculators living before his time. For this reason he takes his place as an originator of a school of thought as well as the leader of a movement looking to a practical end.

As to the motives which drive him and the aspirations which guide him, in destructive criticism and in creative speculation alike, he is primarily a theoretician busied with the analysis of economic phenomena and their organisation into a consistent and faithful system of scientific knowledge; but he is, at the same time, consistently and tenaciously alert to the bearing which each step in the progress of his theoretical work has upon the propaganda. His work has, therefore, an air of bias, such as belongs to an advocate's argument; but it is not, therefore, to be assumed, nor indeed to be credited, that his propagandist aims have in any substantial way deflected his inquiry or his speculations from the faithful pursuit of scientific truth. His socialistic bias may color his polemics, but his logical grasp is too neat and firm to admit of any bias, other than that of his metaphysical preconceptions, affecting his theoretical work.

There is no system of economic theory more logical than that of Marx. No member of the system, no single article of doctrine, is fairly to be understood, criticised, or defended except as an articulate member of the whole and in the light of the preconceptions and postulates which afford the point of departure and the controlling norm of the whole. As regards these preconceptions and postulates, Marx draws on two distinct lines of antecedents,—the Materialistic Hegelianism and the English system of Natural Rights. By his earlier training he is an adept in the Hegelian method of speculation and inoculated with the metaphysics of development underlying the Hegelian system. By his later training he is an expert in the system of Natural Rights and Natural Liberty, ingrained in his ideals of life and held inviolate throughout. He does not take a critical attitude toward the underlying principles of Natural Rights. Even his Hegelian preconceptions of development never carry him the length of questioning the fundamental principles of that system. He is only more ruthlessly consistent in working out their content than his natural-rights antagonists in the liberal-classical school. His polemics run against the specific tenets of the liberal school, but they run wholly on the ground afforded by the premises of that school. The ideals of his propaganda are natural-rights ideals, but his theory of the working out of these ideals in the course of history rests on the Hegelian metaphysics of development, and his method of speculation and construction of theory is given by the Hegelian dialectic.

What first and most vividly centered interest on Marx and his speculations was his relation to the revolutionary socialistic movement; and it is those features of his doctrines which bear immediately on the propaganda that still continue to hold the attention of the greater number of his critics. Chief among these doctrines, in the apprehension of his critics, is the theory of value, with its corollaries: (*a*) the doctrines of the exploitation of labor by capital; and (*b*) the laborer's claim to the whole product of his labor. Avowedly, Marx traces his doctrine of labor-value to Ricardo, and through him to the classical economists. The laborer's claim to the whole product of labor, which is pretty constantly implied, though not frequently avowed by Marx, he has in all probability taken from English writers of the early nineteenth century, more particularly from William Thompson. These doctrines are, on their face, nothing but a development of the conceptions of natural rights which then pervaded English speculation and afforded the metaphysical ground of the liberal movement. The more formidable critics of the Marxian socialism have made much of these doctrinal elements that further the propaganda, and have, by laying the stress on these, diverted attention from other elements that are of more vital consequence to the system as a body of theory. Their exclusive interest in this side of "scientific socialism" has even led them to deny the Marxian system all substantial originality, and make it a (doubtfully legitimate) offshoot of English Liberalism and natural rights. But this is one-sided criticism. It may hold as against certain tenets of the so-called "scientific socialism," but it is not altogether to the point as regards the Marxian system of theory. Even the Marxian theory of value, surplus value, and exploitation, is not simply the doctrine of William Thompson, transcribed and sophisticated in a forbidding terminology, however great the superficial resemblance and however large Marx's unacknowledged debt to Thompson may be on these heads. For many details and for much of his animus Marx may be indebted to the Utilitarians; but, after all, his system of theory, taken as a whole, lies within the frontiers of neo-Hegelianism, and even the details are worked out in accord with the preconceptions of that school of thought and have taken on the complexion that would properly belong to them on that ground. It is, therefore, not by an itemised scrutiny of the details of doctrine and by tracing their pedigree in detail that a fair conception of Marx and his contribution to economics may be reached, but rather by following him from his own point of departure out into the ramifications of his theory, and so overlooking the whole in the prespective which the lapse of time now affords us, but which he could not himself attain, since he was too near to his own work to see why he went about it as he did.

The comprehensive system of Marxism is comprised within the scheme of the Materialistic Conception of History. This materialistic conception is essentially Hegelian, although it belongs with the Hegelian Left, and its immediate affiliation is with Feuerbach, not with the direct line of Hegelian orthodoxy. The chief point of interest here, in identifying the materialistic conception with Hegelianism, is that this identification throws it immediately and uncompromisingly into contrast with Darwinism and the post-Darwinian conceptions of evolution. Even if a plausible English pedigree should be worked out for this Materialistic Conception, or "Scientific Socialism," as has been attempted, it remains none the less true that the conception with which Marx went to his work was a transmuted framework of Hegelian dialectic.

Roughly, Hegelian materialism differs from Hegelian orthodoxy by inverting the main logical sequence, not by discarding the logic or resorting to new tests of truth or finality. One might say, though perhaps with excessive crudity, that, where Hegel pronounces his dictum, *Das Denken ist das Sein,* the materialists, particularly Marx and Engels, would say *Das Sein macht das Denken.* But in both cases some sort of a creative primacy is assigned to one or the other member of the complex, and in neither case is the relation between the two members a causal relation. In the materialistic conception man's spiritual life—what man thinks—is a reflex of what he is in the material respect, very much in the same fashion as the orthodox Hegelian would make the material world a reflex of the spirit. In both, the dominant norm of speculation and formulation of theory is the conception of movement, development, evolution, progress; and in both the movement is conceived necessarily to take place by the method of conflict or struggle. The movement is of the nature of progress,—gradual advance toward a goal, toward the realisation in explicit form of all that is implicit in the substantial activity involved in the movement. The movement is, further, self-conditioned and self-acting: it is an unfolding by inner necessity. The struggle which constitutes the method of movement or evolution is, in the Hegelian system proper, the struggle of the spirit for self-realisation by the process of the well-known three-phase dialectic. In the materialistic conception of history this dialectical movement becomes the class struggle of the Marxian system.

The class struggle is conceived to be "material," but the term "material" is in this connection used in a metaphorical sense. It does not mean mechanical or physical, or even physiological, but economic. It is material in the sense that it is a struggle between classes for the material means of life. "The materialistic conception of history proceeds on the principle that production and, next to production, the exchange of its products is the groundwork of every social order." The social order takes its form through the class struggle, and the character of the class struggle at any given phase of the unfolding development of society is determined by "the prevailing mode of economic production and exchange." The dialectic of the movement of social progress, therefore, moves on the spiritual plane of human desire and passion, not on the (literally) material plane of mechanical and physiological stress, on which the developmental process of brute creation unfolds itself. It is a sublimated materialism, sublimated by the dominating presence of the conscious human spirit; but it is conditioned by the material facts of the production of the means of life. The ultimately active forces involved in the process of unfolding social life are (apparently) the material agencies engaged in the mechanics of production; but the dialectic of the process—the class struggle—runs its course only among and in terms of the secondary (epigenetic) forces of human consciousness engaged in the valuation of the material products of industry. A consistently materialistic conception, consistently adhering to a materialistic interpretation of the process of development as well as of the facts involved in the process, could scarcely avoid making its putative dialectic struggle a mere unconscious and irrelevant conflict of the brute material forces. This would have amounted to an interpretation in terms of opaque cause and effect, without recourse to the concept of a conscious class struggle, and it might have led to a concept of evolution similar to the unteleological Darwinian concept of natural selection. It could scarcely have led to the Marxian notion of a conscious class struggle as the one necessary method of social progress, though it might conceivably, by the aid of empirical generalisation, have led to a scheme of social process in which a class struggle would be included as an incidental though perhaps highly efficient factor. It would have led, as Darwinism has, to a concept of a process of cumulative change in social structure and function; but this process, being essentially a cumulative sequence of causation, opaque and unteleological, could not, without an infusion of pious fancy by the speculator, be asserted to involve progress as distinct from retrogression or to tend to a "realisation" or "self-realisation" of the human spirit or of anything else. Neither could it conceivably be asserted to lead up to a final term, a goal to which all lines of the process should converge and beyond which the process would not go, such as the assumed goal of the Marxian process of class struggle, which is conceived to cease in the classless economic structure of the socialistic final term. In Darwinism there is no such final or perfect term, and no definitive equilibrium.

The disparity between Marxism and Darwinism, as well as the disparity within the Marxian system between the range of material facts that are conceived to be the fundamental forces of the process, on the one hand, and the range of spiritual facts within which the dialectic movement proceeds,—this disparity is shown in the character assigned the class struggle by Marx and Engels. The struggle is asserted to be a conscious one, and proceeds on a recognition by the competing classes of their mutually incompatible interests with regard to the material means of life. The class struggle proceeds on motives of interest, and a recognition of class interest can, of course, be reached only by reflection on the facts of the case. There is, therefore, not even a direct causal connection between the material forces in the case and the choice of a given interested line of conduct. The attitude of the interested party does not result from the material forces so immediately as to place it within the relation of direct cause and effect, nor even with such a degree of intimacy as to admit of its being classed as a tropismatic, or even instinctive, response to the impact of the material force in question. The sequence of reflection, and the consequent choice of sides to a quarrel, run entirely alongside of a range of material facts concerned.

A further characteristic of the doctrine of class struggle requires mention. While the concept is not Darwinian, it is also not legitimately Hegelian, whether of the Right or the Left. It is of a utilitarian origin and of English pedigree, and it belongs to Marx by virtue of his having borrowed its elements from the system of self-interest. It is in fact a piece of hedonism, and is related to Bentham rather than to Hegel. It proceeds on the grounds of the hedonistic calculus, which is equally foreign to the Hegelian notion of an unfolding process and to the post-Darwinian notions of cumulative causation. As regards the tenability of the doctrine, apart from the question of its derivation and its compatibility with the neo-Hegelian postulates, it is to be added that it is quite out of harmony with the later results of psychological inquiry,—just as is true of the use made of the hedonistic calculus by the classical (Austrian) economics.

Within the domain covered by the materialistic conception, that is to say within the domain of unfolding human culture, which is the field of Marxian speculation at large, Marx has more particularly devoted his efforts to an analysis and theoretical formulation of the present situation,—the current phase of the process, the capitalistic system. And, since the prevailing mode of the production of goods determines the institutional, intellectual, and spiritual life of the epoch, by determining the form and method of the current class struggle, the discussion necessarily begins with the theory of "capitalistic production," or production as carried on under the capitalistic system.[1] Under the capitalistic system, that is to say under the system of modern business traffic, production is a production of commodities, merchantable goods, with a view to the price to be obtained for them in the market. The great fact on which all industry under this system hinges is the price of marketable goods. Therefore it is at this point that Marx strikes into the system of capitalistic production, and therefore the theory of value becomes the dominant feature of his economics and the point of departure for the whole analysis, in all its voluminous ramifications.[2]

[1] It may be noted, by way of caution to readers familiar with the terms only as employed by the classical (English and Austrian) economists, that in Marxian usage "capitalistic production" means production of goods for the market by hired labor under the direction of employers who own (or control) the means of production and are engaged in industry for the sake of a profit. "Capital" is wealth (primarily funds) so employed. In these and other related points of terminological usage Marx is, of course, much more closely in touch with colloquial usage than those economists of the classical line who make capital signify "the products of past industry used as aids to further production." With Marx "Capitalism" implies certain relations of ownership, no less than the "productive use" which is alone insisted on by so many later economists in defining the term.

[2] In the sense that the theory of value affords the point of departure and the fundamental concepts out of which the further theory of the workings of capitalism is constructed,—in this sense, and in this sense only, is the theory of value the central doctrine and the critical tenet of Marxism. It does not follow that the Marxist doctrine of an irresistible drift towards a socialistic consummation hangs on the defensibility of the labor-value theory, nor even that the general structure of the Marxist economics would collapse if translated into other terms than those of this doctrine of labor-value. . . .

It is scarcely worth while to question what serves as the beginning of wisdom in the current criticisms of Marx; namely, that he offers no adequate proof of his labor-value theory. It is even safe to go farther, and say that he offers no proof of it. The feint which occupies the opening paragraphs of the *Kapital* and the corresponding passages of *Zur Kritik*, etc., is not to be taken seriously as an attempt to prove his position on this head by the ordinary recourse to argument. It is rather a self-satisfied superior's playful mystification of those readers (critics) whose limited powers do not enable them to see that his proposition is self-evident. Taken on the Hegelian (neo-Hegelian) ground, and seen in the light of the general materialistic conception, the proposition that value = labor-cost is self-evident, not to say tautological. Seen in any other light, it has no particular force.

In the Hegelian scheme of things the only substantial reality is the unfolding life of the spirit. In the neo-Hegelian scheme, as embodied in the materialistic conception, this reality is translated into terms of the unfolding (material) life of man in society.[3] In so far as the goods are products of industry, they are the output of this unfolding life of man, a material residue embodying a given fraction of this forceful life-process. In this life-process lies all substantial reality, and all finally valid relations of quantivalence between the products of this life-process must run in its terms. The life-process, which, when it takes the specific form of an expenditure of labor power, goes to produce goods, is a process of material forces, the spiritual or mental features of the life-process and of labor being only its insubstantial reflex. It is consequently only in the material changes wrought by this expenditure of labor power that the metaphysical substance of life—labor power—can be embodied; but in these changes of material fact it cannot but be embodied, since these are the end to which it is directed.

This balance between goods in respect of their magnitude as output of human labor holds goods indefeasibly, in point of the metaphysical

[3] In much the same way, and with an analogous effect on their theoretical work, in the preconceptions of the classical (including the Austrian) economists, the balance of pleasure and pain is taken to be the ultimate reality in terms of which all economic theory must be stated and to terms of which all phenomena should finally be reduced in any definitive analysis of economic life. It is not the present purpose to inquire whether the one of these uncritical assumptions is in any degree more meritorious or more serviceable than the other.

reality of the life-process, whatever superficial (phenomenal) variations from this norm may occur in men's dealings with the goods under the stress of the strategy of self-interest. Such is the value of the goods in reality; they are equivalents of one another in the proportion in which they partake of this substantial quality, although their true ratio of equivalence may never come to an adequate expression in the transactions involved in the distribution of the goods. This real or true value of the goods is a fact of production, and holds true under all systems and methods of production, whereas the exchange value (the "phenomenal form" of the real value) is a fact of distribution, and expresses the real value more or less adequately according as the scheme of distribution in force at the given time conforms more or less closely to the equities given by production. If the output of industry were distributed to the productive agents strictly in proportion to their shares in production, the exchange value of the goods would be presumed to conform to their real value. But, under the current, capitalistic system, distribution is not in any sensible degree based on the equities of production, and the exchange value of goods under this system can therefore express their real value only with a very rough, and in the main fortuitous, approximation. Under a socialistic régime, where the laborer would get the full product of his labor, or where the whole system of ownership, and consequently the system of distribution, would lapse, values would reach a true expression, if any.

Under the capitalistic system the determination of exchange value is a matter of competitive profit-making, and exchange values therefore depart erratically and incontinently from the proportions that would legitimately be given them by the real values whose only expression they are. Marx's critics commonly identify the concept of "value" with that of "exchange value," and show that the theory of "value" does not square with the run of the facts of price under the existing system of distribution, piously hoping thereby to have refuted the Marxian doctrine; whereas, of course, they have for the most part not touched it. The misapprehension of the critics may be due to a (possibly intentional) oracular obscurity on the part of Marx. Whether by his fault or their own, their refutations have hitherto been quite inconclusive. Marx's severest stricture on the iniquities of the capitalistic system is that contained by implication in his development of the manner in which actual exchange value of goods systematically diverges from their real (labor-cost) value. Herein, indeed, lies not only the inherent iniquity of the existing system, but also its fateful infirmity, according to Marx.

The theory of value, then, is *contained in* the main postulates of the Marxian system rather than derived from them. Marx identifies this doctrine, in its elements, with the labor-value theory of Ricardo, but the relationship between the two is that of a superficial coincidence in their main propositions rather than a substantial identity of theoretic contents. In Ricardo's theory the source and measure of value is sought in the effort and sacrifice undergone by the producer, consistently, on the whole, with the Benthamite-utilitarian position to which Ricardo somewhat loosely and uncritically adhered. The decisive fact about labor, that quality by virtue of which it is assumed to be the final term in the theory of production, is its irksomeness. Such is of course not the case in the labor-value theory of Marx, to whom the question of the irksomeness of labor is quite irrelevant, so far as regards the relation between labor and production. The substantial diversity or incompatibility of the two theories shows itself directly when each is employed by its creator in the further analysis of economic phenomena. Since with Ricardo the crucial point is the degree of irksomeness of labor, which serves as a measure both of the labor expended and the value produced, and since in Ricardo's utilitarian philosophy there is no more vital fact underlying this irksomeness, therefore no surplus-value theory follows from the main position. The productiveness of labor is not cumulative, in its own working; and the Ricardian economics goes on to seek the cumulative productiveness of industry in the functioning of the products of labor when employed in further production and in the irksomeness of the capitalist's abstinence. From which duly follows the general position of classical economics on the theory of production.

With Marx, on the other hand, the labor power expended in production being itself a product and having a substantial value corresponding to its own labor-cost, the value of the labor power expended and the value of the product created by its expenditure need not be the same. They are not the same, by supposition, as they would be in any hedonistic interpretation of the facts. Hence a discrepancy arises between the value of the labor power expended in production and the value of the product created, and this discrepancy is covered by the concept of surplus value. Under the capitalistic system, wages being the value (price) of the labor power consumed in industry, it follows that the surplus product of their labor cannot go to the laborers, but becomes the profits of capital and the source of its accumulation and increase. From the fact that wages are measured by the value of labor power rather than by the (greater) value of the product of labor, it follows also that the laborers are unable to buy the whole product of their labor, and so that the capitalists are unable to sell the whole product of industry continuously at its full value, whence arise difficulties of the gravest nature in the capitalistic system, in the way of overproduction and the like.

But the gravest outcome of this systematic discrepancy between the value of labor power and the value of its product is the accumulation of capital out of unpaid labor, and the effect of this accumulation on the laboring population. The law of accumulation, with its corollary, the doctrine of the industrial reserve army, is the final term and the objective point of Marx's theory of capitalist production, just as the theory of labor value is his point of departure.[4] While the theory of value and surplus value are Marx's explanation of the possibility of existence of the capitalistic system, the law of the accumulation of capital is his exposition of the causes which must lead to the collapse of that system and of the manner in which the collapse will come. And since Marx is, always and everywhere, a socialist agitator as well as a theoretical economist, it may be said without hesitation that the law of accumulation is the climax of his great work, from whatever point of view it is looked at, whether as an economic theorem or as a tenet of socialistic doctrine.

The law of capitalistic accumulation may be paraphrased as follows: Wages being the (approximately exact) value of the labor power bought in the wage contract; the price of the product being the (similarly approximate) value of the goods produced; and since the value of the product exceeds that of the labor power by a given amount (surplus value), which by force of the wage contract passes into the possession of the capitalist and is by him in part laid by as savings and added to the capital already in hand, it follows (a) that, other

[4] Oppenheimer (*Das Grundgesetz der Marx'schen Gesellschaftslehre*) is right in making the theory of accumulation the central element in the doctrines of Marxist socialism, but it does not follow, as Oppenheimer contends, that this doctrine is the keystone of Marx's economic theories. It follows logically from the theory of surplus value, as indicated above, and rests on that theory in such a way that it would fail (in the form in which it is held by Marx) with the failure of the doctrine of surplus value.

things equal, the larger the surplus value, the more rapid the increase of capital; and, also (*b*), that the greater the increase of capital relatively to the labor force employed, the more productive the labor employed and the larger the surplus product available for accumulation. The process of accumulation, therefore, is evidently a cumulative one; and, also evidently, the increase added to capital is an unearned increment drawn from the unpaid surplus product of labor.

But with an appreciable increase of the aggregate capital a change takes place in its technological composition, whereby the "constant" capital (equipment and raw materials) increases disproportionately as compared with the "variable" capital (wages fund). "Labor-saving devices" are used to a greater extent than before, and labor is saved. A larger proportion of the expenses of production goes for the purchase of equipment and raw materials, and a smaller proportion—though perhaps an absolutely increased amount—goes for the purchase of labor power. Less labor is needed relatively to the aggregate capital employed as well as relatively to the quantity of goods produced. Hence some portion of the increasing labor supply will not be wanted, and an "industrial reserve army," a "surplus labor population," an army of unemployed, comes into existence. This reserve grows relatively larger as the accumulation of capital proceeds and as technological improvements consequently gain ground; so that there result two divergent cumulative changes in the situation,—antagonistic, but due to the same set of forces and, therefore, inseparable: capital increases, and the number of unemployed laborers (relatively) increases also.

This divergence between the amount of capital and output, on the one hand, and the amount received by laborers as wages, on the other hand, has an incidental consequence of some importance. The purchasing power of the laborers, represented by their wages, being the largest part of the demand for consumable goods, and being at the same time, in the nature of the case, progressively less adequate for the purchase of the product, represented by the price of the goods produced, it follows that the market is progressively more subject to glut from overproduction, and hence to commercial crises and depression. It has been argued, as if it were a direct inference from Marx's position, that this maladjustment between production and markets, due to the laborer not getting the full product of his labor, leads directly to the breakdown of the capitalistic system, and so by its own force will bring on the socialistic consummation. Such is not

Marx's position, however, although crises and depression play an important part in the course of development that is to lead up to socialism. In Marx's theory, socialism is to come by way of a conscious class movement on the part of the propertyless laborers, who will act advisedly on their own interest and force the revolutionary movement for their own gain. But crises and depression will have a large share in bringing the laborers to a frame of mind suitable for such a move.

Given a growing aggregate capital, as indicated above, and a concomitant reserve of unemployed laborers growing at a still higher rate, as is involved in Marx's position, this body of unemployed labor can be, and will be, used by the capitalists to depress wages, in order to increase profits. Logically, it follows that, the farther and faster capital accumulates, the larger will be the reserve of unemployed, both absolutely and relatively to the work to be done, and the more severe will be the pressure acting to reduce wages and lower the standard of living, and the deeper will be the degradation and misery of the working class and the more precipitately will their condition decline to a still lower depth. Every period of depression, with its increased body of unemployed labor seeking work, will act to hasten and accentuate the depression of wages, until there is no warrant even for holding that wages will, on an average, be kept up to the subsistence minimum.[5] Marx, indeed, is explicit to the effect that such will be the case,—that wages will decline below the subsistence minimum; and he cites English conditions of child labor, misery, and degeneration to substantiate his views. When this has gone far enough, when capitalist production comes near enough to occupying the whole field of industry and has depressed the condition of its laborers sufficiently to make them an effective majority of the community with nothing to lose, then, having taken advice together, they will move, by legal or extra-legal means, by absorbing the state or by subverting it, to establish the social revolution.

Socialism is to come through class antagonism due to the absence of all property interests from the laboring class, coupled with a generally prevalent misery so profound as to involve some degree of physical degeneration. This misery is to be brought about by the heightened productivity of labor due to an increased accumulation of capital and large improvements in the industrial arts; which in turn

[5] The "subsistence minimum" is here taken in the sense used by Marx and the classical economists, as meaning what is necessary to keep up the supply of labor at its current rate of efficiency.

is caused by the fact that under a system of private enterprise with hired labor the laborer does not get the whole product of his labor; which, again, is only saying in other words that private ownership of capital goods enables the capitalist to appropriate and accumulate the surplus product of labor. As to what the régime is to be which the social revolution will bring in, Marx has nothing particular to say, beyond the general thesis that there will be no private ownership, at least not of the means of production.

Such are the outlines of the Marxian system of socialism. In all that has been said so far no recourse is had to the second and third volumes of *Kapital*. Nor is it necessary to resort to these two volumes for the general theory of socialism. They add nothing essential, although many of the details of the processes concerned in the working out of the capitalist scheme are treated with greater fullness, and the analysis is carried out with great consistency and with admirable results. For economic theory at large these further two volumes are important enough, but an inquiry into their contents in that connection is not called for here.

Nothing much need be said as to the tenability of this theory. In its essentials, or at least in its characteristic elements, it has for the most part been given up by latter-day socialist writers. The number of those who hold to it without essential deviation is growing gradually smaller. Such is necessarily the case, and for more than one reason. The facts are not bearing it out on certain critical points, such as the doctrine of increasing misery; and the Hegelian philosophical postulates, without which the Marxism of Marx is groundless, are for the most part forgotten by the dogmatists of to-day. Darwinism has largely supplanted Hegelianism in their habits of thought.

The particular point at which the theory is most fragile, considered simply as a theory of social growth, is its implied doctrine of population,—implied in the doctrine of a growing reserve of unemployed workmen. The doctrine of the reserve of unemployed labor involves as a postulate that population will increase anyway, without reference to current or prospective means of life. The empirical facts give at least a very persuasive apparent support to the view expressed by Marx, that misery is, or has hitherto been, no hindrance to the propagation of the race; but they afford no conclusive evidence in support of a thesis to the effect that the number of laborers must increase independently of an increase of the means of life. No one since Darwin would have the hardihood to say that the increase of the human species is not conditioned by the means of living.

But all that does not really touch Marx's position. To Marx, the neo-Hegelian history, including the economic development, is the life-history of the human species; and the main fact in this life-history, particularly in the economic aspect of it, is the growing volume of human life. This, in a manner of speaking, is the base-line of the whole analysis of the process of economic life, including the phase of capitalist production with the rest. The growth of population is the first principle, the most substantial, most material factor in this process of economic life, so long as it is a process of growth, of unfolding, of exfoliation, and not a phase of decrepitude and decay. Had Marx found that his analysis led him to a view adverse to this position, he would logically have held that the capitalist system is the mortal agony of the race and the manner of its taking off. Such a conclusion is precluded by his Hegelian point of departure, according to which the goal of the life-history of the race in a large way controls the course of that life-history in all its phases, including the phase of capitalism. This goal or end, which controls the process of human development, is the complete realisation of life in all its fullness, and the realisation is to be reached by a process analogous to the three-phase dialectic, of thesis, antithesis, and synthesis, into which scheme the capitalist system, with its overflowing measure of misery and degradation, fits as the last and most dreadful phase of antithesis. Marx, as a Hegelian,—that is to say, a romantic philosopher,—is necessarily an optimist, and the evil (antithetical element) in life is to him a logically necessary evil, as the antithesis is a necessary phase of the dialectic; and it is a means to the consummation, as the antithesis is a means to the synthesis.

5

Imperial Germany and the Industrial Revolution*

This excerpt from a major and much-neglected work of Veblen's is a compact illustration of his method and a sophisticated compendium of his views. It is a closely reasoned chapter of a highly compressed book, Imperial Germany and the Industrial Revolution. *But fundamental issues are broached on nearly every page. There is painstaking attention in this discussion of "the Baltic peoples" to data drawn, with insouciance, from biology, archaeology, history, ethnology, and economics. And there is immediate recourse to theory, i.e., to the broader implications of these data.*

Now and then the reader will be jarred by a false note. But how seldom! He will be much more struck by the freshness of these reflections on cultural and technological borrowing. Aware of the still quite vigorous battle between evolutionism, functionalism, and diffusionism, he cannot but be impressed by Veblen's demonstration that the conflict is an unnatural one. Veblen demonstrates that culture evolves, acculturation takes place, and items of one culture are borrowed by the carriers of another culture and become embedded in a new interdependent whole. This process is both stabilizing and destabilizing. Pushed too far and too fast, it can overwhelm a culture and cause it to collapse. On the other hand, it has many merits, some so great that it can help the borrower to surpass the originator. All of the economically underdeveloped world is a laboratory in which these propositions are now being broadly tested—and substantially verified.

In one connection and another it has already appeared that this stone and bronze-age culture of the Baltic peoples drew for its elements on other cultural regions and earlier phases of civilisation. These peoples borrowed persistently and with great facility. So far as this practice of borrowing is traceable in the stone age it is necessarily a borrowing of technological elements, since the nature of the materials in which they worked has allowed very little but industrial appliances to come down to the present; but as regards these technological elements the borrowing is of the most ubiquitous character. Even in the use of flint, as shown by the series of implements running through the period specifically characterised by the kitchen middens and down over the full-blown neolithic into the bronze age,—even in their use of flint they appear to have learned much of the serviceable innovations from outside, chiefly from the south. The early kitchen-midden implements are rather rudely chipped flints and it is apparent that the grinding of flint was unknown on the Scandinavian waters in that time. Presently, when the use of new and more serviceable forms, such as to suggest that they were worked out by help of examples drawn from the more advanced neolithic populations to the south. But along with a due recognition of this technological indebtedness it is also to be recognised that the Baltic people presently carried this polished (and chipped) flint technology to a perfection of workmanship and mechanical serviceability not surpassed, even if it may have been equalled, by any other neolithic culture.

Again, neither the crop plants nor the domestic animals are visibly present in the kitchen middens from the outset. As for the crop plants this may mean only a quite intelligible failure of evidence, and does not conclusively argue that, e.g., barely was not known and used from the beginning of the Baltic settlement, though the total absence of any trade is not to be set aside as having no significance. For the domestic animals, on the other hand, the negative evidence is conclusive, and it must be taken as an ascertained fact that these were introduced gradually at an appreciable interval after the beginnings of the Baltic culture had been made, and after the Baltic peoples had definitely acquired the (hybrid) racial complexion that marks them through later time. The paucity of the material, not in volume but in range, permits little more to be said in this connection for the stone age; except it be that the only other appreciable material evidence available, that of the graves and mounds, runs to much the same effect,—the use of these being also held to have been learned from outside, and developed in a characteristic manner on lines originally given by the same usage as it prevailed in other countries.

Throughout the bronze and iron periods of prehistory the same facile borrowing goes on; both the use and the material of the bronze and iron work being of foreign derivation. And as the sequence comes on down the ages and approaches historical dates, offering a progressively increasing volume and diversity of archæological material, the evidence of borrowing extends also to other than the industrial arts. As the beginning of history, in the stricter sense, is approached this borrowing shows itself ever more notoriously in the æsthetic arts; in which, at the close of the pagan era, e.g., Scandinavian art shows its indebtedness to the Irish and other Gælic culture at every turn. What is known of late Baltic (mainly Scandinavian) paganism carries the same insidious suggestion of facility for new ideas in the domain of supernatural beliefs; very much as the shifting progression of usages in sepulture in the remoter past argues that these peoples were not above learning from their neighbors, or perhaps rather were temperamentally defenseless against innovation from the outside. In the late pagan era they seem, e.g., to have borrowed, and in some degree made over, several deities of foreign extraction; and it may be recalled that the pagan era closes with the wholesale acceptance of an alien mythology and religious scheme, the improvement and adaptation of which to their own temperamental needs has occupied much of the serious attention of these peoples ever since.

None of this extensive and unremitting draught on the technological and institutional resources of other cultural regions can be called an idle borrowing. The borrowed elements have invariably been assimilated, drawn into the cultural system and so combined and shaped to its purpose as to have led to an unbroken evolution of a scheme peculiar to these (hybrid) peoples and their needs, rather than to the substitution of a scheme from outside or a piecing-out of the scheme of things into which it is intruded. In other words, the borrowing has been done in a thoroughly workmanlike manner and with a free hand.

This proclivity to borrow, and the free and easy efficiency with which borrowed elements are turned to account, is a characteristic trait of north-European antiquity, as, indeed, it is still something of a distinctive mark of these peoples. It probably marks a temperamental bent of the north-European population, at the same time that it gives a certain characteristic flexibility to their scheme of institutions. As a temperamental trait it would appear to be traceable, at least in good part, to the fact of their hybrid extraction; possibly also in part to the peculiar race characteristics of the stocks from which this hybrid population is derived.[1]

The efficacy of borrowing that so comes to light in the life-history of the Baltic culture, as also in a less notorious manner in other instances of cultural intercourse, puts up to the student of institutions a perplexing question, or rather a group of perplexing questions. Something has just been said on the question of why one people borrows elements of culture or of technology with greater facility and effect than another. But the larger question stands untouched: Why do the borrowed elements lend themselves with greater facility and effect to their intrinsic use in the hands of the borrower people than in the hands of the people to whose initiative they are due? Why are borrowed elements of culture more efficiently employed than home-grown innovations? or more so than the same elements at the hands of their originators? It would of course be quite bootless to claim that such is always or necessarily the case, but it is likewise not to be denied that, as a matter of history, technological innovations

[1] Certain other cultural regions and populations offer an instructive parallel on this head, notably the Japanese, and possibly also the Aegean peoples of antiquity. Like the Baltic peoples the Japanese are a hybrid population, a composite of two (perhaps rather three) main racial stocks, with two or three minor racial factors thrown in. Such has apparently been the composition of the Japanese population since the first beginnings of which anything can be said to be known, even if the legends of the *Ko Ji Ki*—the "Records of Ancient Matters"—be accepted at what may be called their face value. By a curious coincidence, the period of Japanese prehistory and history seems to cover loosely the same general interval of time as that of the Baltic peoples; and as with the latter, so in the case of the Japanese, the cultural life-history of the people is a history of facile and ubiquitous borrowing done in the most workmanlike manner and executed with the most serviceable effect. The instance of Japan, however, palpably suggests that this temperamental facility for the acceptance and utilisation of cultural elements from outside, whether in the Japanese or in the Baltic population, should be credited not so much to any marked racial traits of temperament in the constituents of such a hybrid people, but rather to the fact of hybrid derivation itself. It would seem to be due in great part to the exceptionally wide range of variation among the individuals of such a hybrid people, quite as much as to any presumed exceptional facility of this kind in any one of the racial types that have gone to make up the composite population. The parallel between the Japanese and the Baltic peoples in this respect can by no stretch of fantastic ethnological argument be set down to a putative community of descent.

and creations of an institutional nature have in many cases reached their fullest serviceability only at the hands of other communities and other peoples than those to whom these cultural elements owed their origin and initial success. That such should ever be the case is a sufficiently striking phenomenon,—one might even say a sufficiently striking discrepancy.

An explanation, good as far as it goes, though it may not go all the way, is to be looked for in the peculiar circumstances attending the growth, as well as the eventual transmission by borrowing, of any article of the institutional equipment. Technological elements affecting the state of the industrial arts, as being the more concrete and more tangible, will best serve to demonstrate the proposition. Any far-reaching innovation or invention, such as may eventually find a substantial place in the inventory of borrowed elements, will necessarily begin in a small way, finding its way into use and wont among the people where it takes its rise rather tentatively and by tolerance than with a sweeping acceptance and an adequate realisation of its uses and ulterior consequences. Such will have been the case, e.g., with the domestication of the crop plants and the beginnings of tillage, or the domestication of the useful animals, or the use of the metals, or, again, with the rise of the handicraft system, or the industrial revolution that brought in the machine industry. The innovation finds its way into the system of use and wont at the cost of some derangement to the system, provokes to new usages, conventions, beliefs, and principles of conduct, in part directed advisedly to its utilisation or to the mitigation of its immediate consequences, or to the diversion of its usufruct to the benefit of given individuals or classes; but in part there also grow up new habits of thought due to the innovation which it brings into the routine of life, directly in the way of new requirements of manipulation, surveillance, attendance or seasonal time-schedule, and indirectly by affecting the economic relations between classes and localities, as well as the distribution and perhaps the aggregate supply of consumable wealth.

In the early times, such as would come immediately in question here, it is a virtual matter-of-course that any material innovation, or indeed any appreciable unit of technological ways and means, will be attended with a fringe of magical or superstitious conceits and observances. The evidences of this are to be found in good plenty in all cultures, ancient or contemporary, on the savage and barbarian levels; and indeed they are not altogether wanting in civilised life. Many students of ethnology, folk-psychology and religion have busied themselves to good effect with collecting and analysing such material afforded by magical and superstitious practice, and in most instances they are able to trace these practices to some ground of putative utility, connecting them with the serviceable working of the arts of life at one point or another, or with the maintenance of conditions conducive to life and welfare in some essential respect. Where the ethnologist is unable to find such a line of logical connection between superstitious practice and the exigencies of life and welfare, he commonly considers that he has not been able to find what is in the premises, not that the premises do not contain anything of the kind he is bound to expect. But if magical and superstitious practices, or such of them as are at all of material consequence, are with virtual universality to be traced back through the channels of habituation to some putative ground of serviceability for human use, it follows that the rule should work, passably at least, the other way; that the state of the industrial arts which serve human use in such a culture will be shot through with magical and superstitious conceits and observances having an indispensable but wholly putative efficacy.

In many of the lower cultures, or perhaps rather in such of the lower cultures as are at all well known, the workday routine of getting a living is encumbered with a ubiquitous and pervasive scheme of such magical or superstitious conceits and observances, which are felt to constitute an indispensable part of the industrial processes in which they mingle. They embody the putatively efficacious immaterial constituent of all technological procedure; or, seen in detail, they are the spiritual half that completes and animates any process or device throughout its participation in the industrial routine. Like the technological elements with which they are associated, and concomitantly with them, these magically efficacious devices have grown into the prevalent habits of thought of the population and have become an integral part of the common-sense notion of how these technological elements are and are to be turned to account. And at a slightly farther shift in the current of sophistication, out of the same penchant for anthropomorphic interpretation and analogy, a wide range of religious observances, properly so called, will also presently come to bear on the industrial process and the routine of economic life; with a proliferous growth of ceremonial, of propitiation and avoidance, designed to further the propitious course of things to be done.

These matters of the magical and religious ritual of industry and economic arrangements among the peoples of the lower cultures are sufficiently familiar to all ethnological students, and probably they also are so far a matter of common notoriety that there is no need of insistence on their place and value in these lower cultures. They are spoken of here only to recall the fact that the large and consequential technological elements involved in any primitive system of industry have commonly carried such a fringe of putatively efficacious, though mechanically futile, waste motion. These naive forms of mandatory futility are believed to belong only on the lower levels of culture, although it should not be overlooked that magical and religious conceits still exercise something of an inhibitory influence in the affairs of industry even among the very enlightened peoples of Christendom.

But aside from these simple-minded institutional inhibitions on industrial efficiency that seem so much a matter of course in the lower cultures, there are others that run to much the same effect and hold their place among the more enlightened peoples in much the same matter-of-course way. These are in part rather obscure, not having been much attended to in popular speculation, and in part quite notorious, having long been subjects of homiletical iteration. And since this growth of what may be called secular, as contrasted with magical or religious, institutional inhibitions on efficiency, has much to do with latterday economic affairs, as well as with the material fortunes of our prehistoric forebears, a more detailed exposition of their place in economic life will be in place.

On the adoption of new industrial ways and means, whether in the way of specific devices and expedients or of comprehensive changes in methods and processes, there follows a growth of conventional usages governing the utilisation of the new ways and means. This applies equally whether the new expedients are home-bred innovations or technological improvements borrowed from outside; and in any case such a growth of conventions takes time, being of the nature of adaptive habituation. A new expedient, in the way of material appliances or of improved processes, comes into the industrial system and is adapted to the requirements of the state of things into which it is introduced. Certain habitual ways of utilising the new device come to be accepted; as, would happen, e.g., on the introduction of domestic animals among a people previously living by tillage alone and having no acquaintance with the use of such animals under other conditions than those prevailing among purely pastoral peoples.

So, again, the gradual improvement of boat-building and navigation, such as took place among the prehistoric Baltic peoples, would induce a progressive change in the conventional scheme of life and bring on a specialisation of occupations, with some division of economic and social classes. Or, again, in such a large systematic shift as is involved in the coming of the handicraft industry and its spread and maturing; class distinctions, occupational divisions, standardisation of methods and products, together with trade relations and settled markets and trade routes, came gradually into effect. In part these conventional features resulting from and answering to the new industrial factors continued to have the force of common-sense conventional arrangement only; in part they also acquired the added stability given by set agreement, authoritative control and statutory enactment.

So, in the case of the handicraft system such matters as trade routes, methods of package, transportation and consignment, credit relations, and the like, continued very largely, though not wholly nor throughout the vogue of the system, to be regulated by conventional vogue rather than by authoritative formulation; while on the other hand the demarkation between crafts and classes of craftsmen, as well as the standardisation of methods and output, were presently, in the common run, brought under rigorous surveillance by authorities vested with specific powers and acting under carefully formulated rules.

But whether this standardisation and conventionalisation takes the set form of authoritative agreement and enactment or is allowed to rest on the looser ground of settled use and wont, it is always of the nature of a precipitate of past habituation, and is designed to meet exigencies that have come into effect in past experience; it always embodies something of the principle of the dead hand; and along with all the salutary effects of stability and harmonious working that may be credited to such systematisation, it follows also that these standing conventions out of the past unavoidably act to retard, deflect or defeat adaptation to new exigencies that arise in the further course. Conventions that are in some degree effete continue to cumber the ground.

All this apparatus of conventions and standard usage, whether it takes the simpler form of use and wont or the settled character of legally competent enactment and common-law rule, necessarily has trial arts, and so necessarily acts in some degree to lower the net something of this effect of retardation in any given state of the indus-

efficiency of the industrial system which it pervades. But this work of retardation is also backed by the like character attaching to the material equipment by use of which the technological proficiency of the community takes effect. The equipment is also out of the past, and it too lies under the dead hand. In a general way, any minor innovation in processes or in the extension of available resources, or in the scale of organisation, is taken care of as far as may be by a patchwork improvement and amplification of the items of equipment already in hand; the fashion of plant and appliances already in use is adhered to, with concessions in new installations, but it is adhered to more decisively so in any endeavor to bring the equipment in hand up to scale and grade. Changes so made are in part of a concessive nature, in sufficiently large part, indeed, to tell materially on the aggregate; and the fact of such changes being habitually made in a concessive spirit so lessens the thrust in the direction of innovation that even the concessions do not carry as far as might be.[2]

[2] An illustrative instance of this obsolescence of equipment on a large scale and in modern circumstances is afforded by several of the underlying companies of the United States Steel Corporation. The plants in question had been installed at a period when the later methods of steel production had not been perfected and before the later and richer sources of raw materials had become available by the latest methods of transportation; they were also located with a view to smaller markets, distributed on an earlier and now obsolete plan, which has become obsolete through changes in the railway system and the growth of new centers of population. It was technologically impossible to bring them up to date as independent industrial plants, and as a business proposition it was impracticable abruptly to discard them and replace them by new equipment placed to better advantage and organised on a scale to take full advantage of available resources and methods. The remedy sought in the formation of the Steel Corporation was a compromise, whereby the obsolete items of equipment—in part obsolete only in the geographical sense that the industrial situation had shifted out of their way—were gradually discarded and replaced with new plant designed for specialised lines of production, at the same time that the monopolistic position of the new Corporation enabled the shift to be made at a sufficiently slow rate to mask the substitution and make the community at large pay for this temporary lower efficiency due to a gradual disuse of obsolete equipment and methods, in place of such an abrupt and sweeping shift to a new basis as the altered technological situation called for.

At a later juncture the Steel Corporation found itself also face to face with a serious difficulty due to "obsolescence through improvement" of the same general kind; when it appeared that by the later improved processes steel of the first quality could be made from ore peculiar to the southern field as cheaply as from the Minnesota supply on which the Corporation's mills were in the habit of depending, and with special advantages of access to certain markets. How far the

It is in the relatively advanced stages of the industrial arts that this retardation due to use and wont, as distinguished from magical and religious waste and inhibitions on innovation, become of grave consequence. There appears, indeed, to be in some sort a systematic symmetry or balance to be observed in the way in which the one of these lines of technological inhibition comes into effectual bearing as fast as the other declines. At the same time, as fast as commercial considerations, considerations of investment, come to rule industry, the investor's interest comes also to exercise an inhibitory surveillance over technological efficiency, both by the well-known channel of limiting the output and holding up the price to what the traffic will bear,—that is to say what it will bear in the pecuniary sense of yielding the largest net gain to the business men in interest,—and also by the less notorious reluctance of investors and business concerns to replace obsolete methods and plant with new and more efficient equipment.

Beyond these simple and immediate inhibitory convolutions within the industrial system itself, there lies a fertile domain of conventions and institutional arrangements induced as secondary consequences of the growth of industrial efficiency and contrived to keep its net serviceability in bounds, by diverting its energies to industrially unproductive uses and its output to unproductive consumption.

With any considerable advance in the industrial arts business enterprise presently takes over the control of the industrial process; with the consequence that the net pecuniary gain to the business man in control becomes the test of industrial efficiency. This may result in a speeding up of the processes of industry, as is commonly noted by economists. But it also results in "unemployment" whenever a sustained working of the forces engaged does not, or is not believed to, conduce to the employer's largest net gain, as may notoriously happen in production for a market. Also, it follows that industry is controlled and directed with a view to sales, and a wise expenditure of industrial efficiency, in the business sense, comes to mean such expenditure as contributes to sales; which may often mean that the larger share of costs, as the goods reach their users, is the industrially wasteful cost of advertising and other expedients of salesmanship.

The normal result of business control in industry—normal in the

---

resulting acquisition of the southern coal, ore and lime by the Corporation may have resulted in a retardation of efficiency in steel production would be hazardous to guess.

sense of being uniformly aimed at and also in that it commonly follows—is the accumulation of wealth and income in the hands of a class. Under the well-accepted principle of "conspicuous waste" wealth so accumulated is to be put in evidence in visible consumption and visible exemption from work. So that with due, but ordinarily not a large, lapse of time, an elaborate scheme of properties establishes itself, bearing on this matter of conspicuous consumption, so contrived as to "take up the slack." This system of conspicuous waste is a scheme of properties, decencies, and standards of living, the economic motive of which is competitive spending. It works out in a compromise between the immediate spending of income on conspicuous consumption—together with the conspicuous avoidance of industrial work—on the one side, and deferred spending—commonly called "saving"—on the other side. The deferred spending may be deferred to a later day in the lifetime of the saver, or to a later generation; its effects are substantially the same in either case. There is the further reservation to be noted, that in so far as property rights, tenures and the conjunctures of business gain are in any degree insecure, measures will be taken to insure against the risks of loss and eventual inability to keep up appearances according to the accepted standard of living. This insurance takes the shape of accumulation, in one form or another,—provision for future revenue.

Like other conventions and institutional regulations, the scheme of spending rests on current, *i.e.*, immediately past, experience, and as was noted above it is so contrived as to take up the calculable slack,—the margin between production and productive consumption. It is perhaps needless to enter the caution that such a scheme of conspicuous waste does not always, perhaps not in the common run of cases, go to the full limit of what the traffic will bear; but it is also to be noted that it will sometimes, and indeed not infrequently, exceed that limit. Perhaps in all cases, but particularly where the industrial efficiency of the community is notably high, so as to yield a very appreciable margin between productive output and necessary current consumption, some appreciable thought has to be spent on the question of ways and means of spending; and a technique of consumption grows up.

It will be appreciated how serious a question this may become, of the ways and means of reputable consumption, when it is called to mind that in the communities where the modern state of the industrial arts has adequately taken effect this margin of product disposable for wasteful consumption will always exceed fifty per cent of the current product, and will in the more fortunate cases probably exceed seventy-five per cent of the whole. So considerable a margin is not to be disposed of to good effect by haphazard impulse. The due absorption of it in competitive spending takes thought, skill and time for the organisation of ways and means. It is also not a simple problem of conspicuously consuming time and substance, without more ado; men's sense of fitness and beauty requires that the spending should take place in an appropriate manner, such as will not offend good taste and not involve an odiously aimless ostentation. And it takes time and habituation, as well as a discriminate balancing of details, before a scheme of reputable standardised waste is perfected; of course, it also costs time and specialised effort to take due care of the running adjustment of such a scheme to current conditions of taste, ennui and consumptive distinction,—as seen, e.g., in the technique of fashions. It has, indeed, proved to be a matter of some difficulty, not to say of serious strain, in the industrially advanced communities, to keep the scheme of conspicuous waste abreast of the times; so that, besides the conspicuous consumers in their own right, there have grown up an appreciable number of special occupations devoted to the technical needs of reputable spending. The technology of wasteful consumption is large and elaborate and its achievements are among the monuments of human initiative and endeavor; it has its victories and its heroes as well as the technology of production.

But any technological scheme is more or less of a balanced system, in which the interplay of parts has such a character of mutual support and dependence that any substantial addition or subtraction at any one point will involve more or less of derangement all along the line. Neither can an extremely large contingent of reputable waste be suddenly superinduced in the accepted standard of living of any given community—though this difficulty is not commonly a sinister one—nor can a large retrenchment in this domain of what is technically called "the moral standard of living" be suddenly effected without substantial hardship or without seriously disturbing the spiritual balance of the community. To realise the import of such disturbance in the scheme of wasteful consumption one need only try to picture the consternation that would, e.g., fall on the British community consequent on the abrupt discontinuance of the Court and its social and civil manifestations, or of horseracing, or of the established church, or of evening dress.

But since the growth and acceptance of any scheme of wasteful expenditure is after all subsequent to and consequent upon the surplus productivity of the industrial system on which it rests, the introduction, in whole or in part, of a new and more efficient state of the industrial arts does not carry with it from the outset a fully developed system of standardised consumption; particularly, it need not follow that the standard scheme of consumption will be carried over intact in case a new industrial technology is borrowed. There is no intimate or intrinsic mutuality of mechanical detail between the technology of industry and the technique of conspicuous waste; the high-heeled slipper and the high-wrought "picture hat," e.g., are equally well accepted in prehistoric Crete and in twentieth-century France; and the Chinese lady bandages her foot into deformity where the Manchu lady, in evidence of the same degree of opulence in the same town, is careful to let her foot run loose. It is only that, human nature being what it is, a disposable margin of production will, under conditions of private ownership, provoke a competent scheme of wasteful consumption.

Owing to this mechanical discontinuity between any given state of the industrial arts and the scheme of magical, religious, conventional, or pecuniary use and wont with which it lives in some sort of symbiosis, the carrying-over of such a state of the industrial arts from one community to another need not involve the carrying-over of this its spiritual complement. Such is particularly the case where the borrowing takes place across a marked cultural frontier, in which case it follows necessarily that the alien scheme of conventions will not be taken over intact in taking over an alien technological system, whether in whole or in part. The borrowing community or cultural group is already furnished with its own system of conceits and observances—in magic, religion, propriety, and any other line of conventional necessity—and the introduction of a new scheme, or the intrusion of new and alien elements into the accredited scheme already in force, is a work of habituation that takes time and special provocation. All of which applies with added force to the introduction of isolated technological elements from an alien culture, still more particularly, of course, where the technological expedients borrowed are turned to other uses and utilised by other methods than those employed in the culture from which they were borrowed,—as, e.g., would be the case in the acquisition of domestic cattle by a sedentary farming community from a community of nomadic or half-nomadic pastoral people, as appears to have happened in the prehistoric culture of the Baltic peoples. The interposition of a linguistic frontier between the borrower and creditor communities would still farther lessen the chance of immaterial elements of culture being carried over in the transmission of technological knowledge. The borrowed elements of industrial efficiency would be stripped of their fringe of conventional inhibitions and waste, and the borrowing community would be in a position to use them with a freer hand and with a better chance of utilising them to their full capacity, and also with a better chance of improving on their use, turning them to new uses, and carrying the principles (habits of thought) involved in the borrowed items out, with unhampered insight, into farther ramifications of technological proficiency. The borrowers are in a position of advantage, intellectually, in that the new expedient comes into their hands more nearly in the shape of a theoretical principle applicable under given physical conditions; rather than in the shape of a concrete expedient applicable within the limits of traditional use, personal, magical, conventional. It is, in other words, taken over in a measure without the defects of its qualities.

Here, again, is a secondary effect of borrowing, that may not seem of first-rate consequence but is none the less necessarily to be taken into account. The borrowed elements are drawn into a cultural scheme in which they are aliens and into the texture of which they can be wrought only at the cost of some, more or less serious, derangement of the accustomed scheme of life and the accepted system of knowledge and belief. Habituation to their use and insight into their working acts in its degree to incapacitate the borrowers for holding all their home-bred conceits and beliefs intact and in full conviction. They are vehicles of cultural discrepancy, conduce to a bias of skepticism, and act, in their degree, to loosen the bonds of authenticity. Incidentally, the shift involved in such a move will have its distasteful side and carry its burden of disturbance and discomfort; but the new elements, it is presumed, will make their way, and the borrowing community will make its peace with them on such terms as may be had; that assumption being included in the premises.

In some instances of such communication of alien technological and other cultural elements the terms on which a settlement has been effected have been harsh enough, as, e.g., on the introduction of iron tools and fire-arms among the American Indians, or the similar introduction of distilled spirits, of the horse, and of trade—especially in furs—among the same general group of peoples. Polynesia, Australia, and other countries new to the European technology, and to the European conceits and conceptions in law, religion and morals, will be called to mind to the same effect. In these cases the intrusion of alien, but technologically indefeasible, elements of culture has been too large to allow the old order to change; so it has gone to pieces. This result may, of course, have been due in part to a temperamental incapacity of these peoples for the acquisition of new and alien habits of thought; they may not have been good borrowers, at least they appear not to have been sufficiently good borrowers. The same view, in substance, is often formulated to the effect that these are inferior or "backward" races, being apparently not endowed with the traits that conduce to a facile apprehension of the modern European technological system.

It appears to have been otherwise with the peoples of the Baltic culture, late and early. They have been good borrowers, having borrowed persistently, ubiquitously and well. The proof of their exceptional capacity as borrowers is the general run of the life-history of these populations and their culture. As a general proposition, they appear not to have suffered a disproportionate setback in population or in productive efficiency even at those epochs when the borrowing took on a wholesale character, as, e.g., on the transition to bronze, or later to iron, or later still in the sweeping shift from paganism to Christianity. In each of these instances, of course, something of a serious disturbance and impairment is traceable, at least in the two latter episodes; but even the shift to the Christian faith appears to have involved only a relatively transient decline, and in each case this cultural region comes out of the era of transition apparently stronger than before the intrusion of new cultural elements took place. As would be expected, the last named, the shift to Christianity, was the most demoralising of these adventures in cultural borrowing; since this was, in the main and immediately, a borrowing of immaterial, institutional elements, without any corresponding gain in technology; so that in this instance the shock to the cultural scheme came from factors which did not carry such an immediate and intrinsic compensation for the resulting derangement as did the technological change involved in the introduction of the metals. It is, of course, also possible to overstate both the magnitude and the abruptness of the change from the pagan to the Christian scheme in the Baltic region; indeed, it has not been unusual to do so. But when all is said the fact remains that through all their borrowing of expedients, information, institutions and ideals no collapse has overtaken this culture, such as either to reduce the population to virtual extinction—as has happened in analogous circumstances, e.g., in Tasmania, Australia, various parts of Polynesia and America, in a more or less sweeping fashion—or to substitute a substantially alien cultural scheme for what prevailed before the coming of the innovation in technology or in use and wont.

Not that there have been no serious, or even alarming, conjunctures in the cultural history of the Baltic peoples; it is only that they have come through without that degree of discontinuity that would involve a substitution of a new race (or racial mixture) or a new scheme of civilisation alien to what went before. There is at least one juncture in the bronze age when the derangement of the conditions of life in the Baltic country appears to have fallen into really precarious shape,—between the second and third periods of the bronze age in Montelius's chronology, or between the "early" and the "late" bronze age as more commonly spoken of,—and there is suggestive evidence of something of a break at a later point in the sequence, before the coming of iron. Something of grave import, in the way of a difficult interval, may also be surmised in the earlier half of the iron age. What may have been the nature of these episodes that so have an untoward look is at the best a matter of surmise, with little chance of reaching anything like a secure conclusion in the present state of the archæological evidence. There may have been something like hostile contact with alien peoples outside, or internal dissensions, or an epidemic disease, such, e.g., as the black death, or the plague that visited Athens in the fifth century; or it may conceivably have been nothing more serious than an interruption of trade relations with the Mediterraneon and Black Sea, due to extensive raiding or to the shifting of peoples in the intervening territory. Through it all, however, the continuity of the cultural sequence is visible, as is also the efficiency of this culture, in the biological sense that the population does not seriously or enduringly fall off. The latter test is perhaps the more conclusive. So much so that the Baltic region is known to antiquity as a "cradle of nations" even before anything much else is known of it by these civilised peoples of antiquity and their writers.

That it deserved that name and continued to make it good is seen in the inexhaustible barbarian migrations that continued to run outward from the Baltic center.

The presumptive characteristics of this culture, then, as one gets an impression from a study of its antiquities and by inference from the conditions of life which the country offers and from the make-up of its population, may tentatively be set down. It would be a small-scale culture, in the sense that the local units would be of no great magnitude; although it may be conceived to have covered a relatively extensive area in the aggregate and to have covered this area with a fairly dense population; it habitually stood in fairly close communication with other peoples outside, even over relatively long distances, principally by way of trade; these peoples borrowed freely, both in technological and in other institutional matters,[3] and made notably free and efficient use of all borrowed elements. The scheme of institutions, economic, civil, domestic and religious, that would fit these circumstances would be of a relatively slight fixity, flexible, loose-knit, and naive, in the sense that they would be kept in hand under discretionary control of neighborly common sense,—the continued borrowing and the facility with which borrowed elements are assimilated and turned to account goes far to enforce this conclusion. Altogether its most impressive traits are a certain industrial efficiency, particularly efficiency in the mechanic arts, and its conduciveness to the multiplication of its people; whereas its achievements in political organisation or in the domain of art and religion are relatively slight. It is a civilisation of workmanship and fecundity rather than of dynastic power, statecraft, priestcraft or artistic achievement.

[3] In methods of burial, art motives, etc.

6

The Intellectual Pre-eminence of Jews in Modern Europe*

There would be no point in resurrecting an obscure article of Veblen's written in 1919 that dealt only with Zionism. However, the question of establishing a Jewish homeland in Palestine is only superficially the subject matter of "The Intellectual Pre-eminence of Jews in Modern Europe." Veblen could scarcely have been more enthusiastic about Jewish nationalism than about any other kind. It came too late. Large-scale enterprise and universal intercourse made the idea of creating a "self-contained" state, especially such a small one, into a kind of make-believe. The notion of projecting yet another "independent" territory bounded by national frontiers Veblen naturally found unacceptable. Yet he was gentler than usual in the following treatment of a favorite theme, probably because of his own empathy for a persecuted people. He understood their peculiar position.

And he understood it in part because it was so much like his own. There can be no doubt that Veblen strongly identified with the Jew who "becomes a disturber of the intellectual peace" and pays the price as he becomes a "wayfaring man, a wanderer in the intellectual's no-man's-land, seeking another place to rest, farther along the road, somewhere over the horizon." In skillfully depicting the Jew, Veblen also described himself.

There is thus in this essay a second layer of meaning. We may even add a third. For if Veblen felt the painful side of marginality such as his own or that of the Jews, he also knew that being "in" but not "of" one's culture had certain advantages. He spelled out these advantages (as well as Georg Simmel did in his reflections on

* From *Political Science Quarterly,* Vol. XXXIV (March, 1919).

"The Stranger"), and by so doing he gave us a general insight into the contemplative, creative, intellectual life.

Among all the clamorous projects of national self-determination which surround the return of peace, the proposal of the Zionists is notable for sobriety, good will, and a poise of self-assurance. More confidently and perspicuously than all the others, the Zionists propose a rehabilitation of their national integrity under a régime of live and let live, "with charity for all, with malice toward none." Yet it is always a project for withdrawal upon themselves, a scheme of national demarcation between Jew and gentile; indeed, it is a scheme of territorial demarcation and national frontiers of the conventional sort, within which Jews and Jewish traits, traditions, and aspirations are to find scope and breathing space for a home-bred culture and a free unfolding of all that is best and most characteristic in the endowment of the race. There runs through it all a dominant bias of isolation and inbreeding, and a confident persuasion that this isolation and inbreeding will bring great and good results for all concerned. The Zionists aspire to bring to full fruition all that massive endowment of spiritual and intellectual capacities of which their people have given evidence throughout their troubled history, and not least during these concluding centuries of their exile.

The whole project has an idyllic and engaging air. And any disinterested bystander will be greatly moved to wish them godspeed. Yet there comes in a regret that this experiment in isolation and inbreeding could not have been put to the test at an earlier date, before the new order of large-scale industry and universal intercourse had made any conclusive degree of such national isolation impracticable, before this same new order had so shaped the run of things that any nation or community drawn on this small scale would necessarily be dependent on and subsidiary to the run of things at large. It is now, unhappily, true that any "nation" of the size and geographical emplacement of the projected Zion will, for the present and the calculable future, necessarily be something of a national make-believe. The current state of the industrial arts will necessarily deny it a rounded and self-balanced national integrity in any substantial sense. The days of Solomon and the caravan trade which underlay the glory of Solomon are long past.

Yet much can doubtless be done by taking thought and making the most of that spirit of stubborn clannishness which has never been the least among the traits of this people. But again, to any disinterested bystander there will come the question: What is the use of it all? It is not so much a question of what is aimed at, as of the chances of its working-out. The logic of the Zionist project plainly runs to the effect that, whereas this people have achieved great things while living under conditions of great adversity, scattered piecemeal among the gentiles of Europe, they are due to achieve much greater things and to reach an unexampled prosperity so soon as they shall have a chance to follow their own devices untroubled within the shelter of their own frontiers. But the doubt presents itself that the conditioning circumstances are not the same or of the same kind in the occidental twentieth century A.D. as in the oriental twelfth century B.C.; nor need it follow that those things which scattered Jews have achieved during their dispersion among the gentiles of Europe are a safe index of what things may be expected of a nation of Jews turned in upon themselves within the insulating frontiers of the Holy Land. It is on this latter point that a question is raised here as to the nature and causes of Jewish achievement in gentile Europe; and the contrast of the conditions offered by the projected Zion will present itself without argument.

It is a fact which must strike any dispassionate observer that the Jewish people have contributed much more than an even share to the intellectual life of modern Europe. So also it is plain that the civilisation of Christendom continues today to draw heavily on the Jews for men devoted to science and scholarly pursuits. It is not only that men of Jewish extraction continue to supply more than a proportionate quota to the rank and file engaged in scientific and scholarly work, but a disproportionate number of the men to whom modern science and scholarship look for guidance and leadership are of the same derivation. Particularly is this true of the modern sciences, and it applies perhaps especially in the field of scientific theory, even beyond the extent of its application in the domain of workday detail. So much is notorious.

This notable and indeed highly creditable showing has, of course, not escaped the attention of those men of Jewish race who interest themselves in the fortunes of their own people. Not unusually it is set down as a national trait, as evidence of a peculiarly fortunate intellectual endowment, native and hereditary, in the Jewish people. There is much to be said for such a view, but it should not follow that any inquiry into the place and value of the Jewish people in western civilisation should come to rest with this broad assertion of pre-eminence in point of native endowment.

It is true that the history of the Chosen People, late and early, throws them into a position of distinction among the nations with which they have been associated; and it will commonly be accepted without much argument that they have, both late and early, shown distinctive traits of temperament and aptitude, such as to mark them off more or less sharply from all the gentiles among whom it has been their lot to be thrown. So general is the recognition of special Jewish traits, of character and of capacity, that any refusal to recognise something which may be called a Jewish type of hereditary endowment would come to nothing much better than a borrowing of trouble.

That there should be such a tenacious spiritual and intellectual heritage transmissible within the Jewish community and marking that people off in any perceptible degree from their gentile neighbors is all the more notable in view of the known life-history of the children of Israel. No unbiased ethnologist will question the fact that the Jewish people are a nation of hybrids; that gentile blood of many kinds has been infused into the people in large proportions in the course of time. Indeed, none of the peoples of Christendom has been more unremittingly exposed to hybridisation, in spite of all the stiff conventional precautions that have been taken to keep the breed pure. It is not a question of a surreptitious hybrid strain, such as would show itself in sporadic reversions to an alien type; but rather it is a question whether the Jewish strain itself, racially speaking, can at all reasonably be held to account for one half of the pedigree of the Jewish nation as it stands.

The hybrid antecedents of the Children of Israel are not a mere matter of bookish record. Evidence of their hybrid descent is written all over them, wherever they are to be met with, so that in this respect the Jews of Europe are in the same case as the other Europeans, who are also universally cross-bred. It would perplex any anthropologist to identify a single individual among them all who could safely be set down as embodying the Jewish racial type without abatement. The variations in all the measurable traits that go to identify any individual in the schedules of the anthropologists are wide and ubiquitous as regards both their physical and their spiritual traits, in respect of anthropometric measurements as well as in temperament capacities. And yet, when all is said in abatement of it, the Jewish type, it must be admitted, asserts itself with amazing persistence through all the disguises with which it has been overlaid in the course of age-long hybridisation. Whatever may be found true elsewhere, in their contact with other racial types than those of Europe, it still appears that within this European racial environment the outcome given by any infusion of Jewish blood in these cross-bred individuals is something which can be identified as Jewish. Cross-breeding commonly results in a gain to the Jewish community rather than conversely; and the hybrid offspring is a child of Israel rather than of the gentiles.

In effect, therefore, it is the contribution of this Jewish-hybrid people to the culture of modern Europe that is in question. The men of this Jewish extraction count for more than their proportionate share in the intellectual life of western civilisation; and they count particularly among the vanguard, the pioneers, the uneasy guild of pathfinders and iconoclasts, in science, scholarship, and institutional change and growth. On its face it appears as if an infusion of Jewish blood, even in some degree of hybrid attenuation, were the one decisive factor in the case; and something of that sort may well be allowed, to avoid argument if for no more substantial reason. But even a casual survey of the available evidence will leave so broad a claim in doubt.

Of course, there is the fact to be allowed for at the outset, so far as need be, that these intellectuals of Jewish extraction are, after all, of hybrid extraction as well; but this feature of the case need be given no undue weight. It is of consequence in its bearing on the case of the Jews only in the same manner and degree as it is of consequence for any other hybrid people. Cross-breeding gives a wider range of variation and a greater diversity of individual endowment than can be had in any passably pure-bred population; from which results a greater effectual flexibility of aptitudes and capacities in such a people when exposed to conditions that make for change. In this respect the Jews are neither more nor less fortunate than their gentile compatriots.

It may be more to the purpose to note that this intellectual pre-eminence of the Jews has come into bearing within the gentile community of peoples, not from the outside; that the men who have been its bearers have been men immersed in this gentile culture in which they have played their part of guidance and incitement, not bearers of a compelling message from afar or proselyters of enlightenment conjuring with a ready formula worked out in the ghetto and carried over into the gentile community for its mental regeneration. In point of fact, neither these nor other Jews have done effectual missionary work, in any ordinary sense of that term, in this or any other connection; nor have they entertained a design to do so. Indeed, the Chosen People have quite characteristically never been addicted to missionary enterprise; nor does the Jewish scheme of right and honest living comprise anything of the kind. This, too, is notorious fact; so much so that this allusion to it may well strike any Jew as foolish insistence on a commonplace matter of course. In their character of a Chosen People, it is not for them to take thought of their unblest neighbors and seek to dispel the darkness that overlies the soul of the gentiles.

The cultural heritage of the Jewish people is large and rich, and it is of ancient and honorable lineage. And from time immemorial this people has shown aptitude for such work as will tax the powers of thought and imagination. Their home-bred achievements of the ancient time, before the Diaspora, are among the secure cultural monuments of mankind; but these achievements of the Jewish ancients neither touch the frontiers of modern science nor do they fall in the lines of modern scholarship. So also the later achievements of the Jewish scholars and savants, in so far as their intellectual enterprise has gone forward on what may be called distinctively Jewish lines, within the confines of their own community and by the leading of their own home-bred interest, untouched by that peculiar drift of inquiry that characterises the speculations of the modern gentile world—this learning of the later generations of home-bred Jewish scholars is also reputed to have run into lucubrations that have no significance for contemporary science or scholarship at large.

It appears to be only when the gifted Jew escapes from the cultural environment created and fed by the particular genius of his own people, only when he falls into the alien lines of gentile inquiry and becomes a naturalised, though hyphenate, citizen in the gentile republic of learning, that he comes into his own as a creative leader in the world's intellectual enterprise. It is by loss of allegiance, or at the best by force of a divided allegiance to the people of his origin, that he finds himself in the vanguard of modern inquiry.

It will not do to say that none but renegrade Jews count effectually in the modern sciences. Such a statement would be too broad; but, for all its excessive breadth, it exceeds the fact only by a margin. The margin may seem wide, so wide as to vitiate the general statement, perhaps, or at least wide enough materially to reduce its cogency. But it would be wider of the mark to claim that the renegades are to be counted only as sporadic exceptions among a body of unmitigated Jews who make up the virtual total of that muster of creative men of science which the Jewish people have thrown into the intellectual advance of Christendom.

The first requisite for constructive work in modern science, and indeed for any work of inquiry that shall bring enduring results, is a skeptical frame of mind. The enterprising skeptic alone can be counted on to further the increase of knowledge in any substantial fashion. This will be found true both in the modern sciences and in the field of scholarship at large. Much good and serviceable workmanship of a workday character goes into the grand total of modern scientific achievement; but that pioneering and engineering work of guidance, design, and theoretical correlation, without which the most painstaking collection and canvass of information is irrelevant, incompetent, and impertinent—this intellectual enterprise that goes forward presupposes a degree of exemption from hard-and-fast preconceptions, a skeptical animus, *Unbefangenheit*, release from the dead hand of conventional finality.

The intellectually gifted Jew is in a peculiarly fortunate position in respect of this requisite immunity from the inhibitions of intellectual quietism. But he can come in for such immunity only at the cost of losing his secure place in the scheme of conventions into which he has been born, and at the cost, also, of finding no similarly secure place in that scheme of gentile conventions into which he is thrown. For him as for other men in the like case, the skepticism that goes to make him an effectual factor in the increase and diffusion of knowledge among men involves a loss of that peace of mind that is the birthright of the safe and sane quietist. He becomes a disturber of the intellectual peace, but only at the cost of becoming an intellectual wayfaring man, a wanderer in the intellectual no-man's-land, seeking another place to rest, farther along the road, somewhere over the horizon. They are neither a complaisant nor a contented lot, these aliens of the uneasy feet; but that is, after all, not the point in question.

The young Jew who is at all gifted with a taste for knowledge will unavoidably go afield into that domain of learning where the gentile interests dominate and the gentile orientation gives the outcome. There is nowhere else to go on this quest. He comes forthwith to realise that the scheme of traditions and conventional verities handed down within the pale of his own people are matters of habit handed down by tradition, that they have only such force as belongs to matters of habit and convention, and that they lose their binding force so soon as the habitually accepted outlook is given up or seriously deranged. These nationally binding convictions of what is true, good, and beautiful in the world of the human spirit are forthwith seen to be only contingently good and true; to be binding only so far as the habitual will to believe in them and to seek the truth along their lines remains intact. That is to say, only so long as no scheme of habituation alien to the man's traditional outlook has broken in on him, and has forced him to see that those convictions and verities which hold their place as fundamentally and eternally good and right within the balanced scheme of received traditions prove to be, after all, only an ephemeral web of habits of thought; so soon as his current habits of life no longer continue to fall in those traditional lines that keep these habits of thought in countenance.

Now it happens that the home-bred Jewish scheme of things, human and divine, and the ways and means of knowledge that go with such a scheme, are of an archaic fashion, good and true, perhaps, beyond all praise, for the time and conditions that gave rise to it all, that wove that web of habituation and bound its close-knit tissue of traditional vertities and conventions. But it all bears the date-mark, "B.C." It is of a divine complexion, monotheistic even, and perhaps intrinsically thearchic; it is ritualistic, with an exceedingly and beautifully magical efficacy of ritual necessity. It is imperiously self-balanced and self-sufficient, to the point of sanctity; and as is always true of such schemes of sanctity and magical sufficiency, it runs on a logic of personal and spiritual traits, qualities and relations, a class of imponderables which are no longer of the substance of those things that are inquired into by men to whom the ever increasingly mechanistic orientation of the modern time becomes habitual.

When the gifted young Jew, still flexible in respect of his mental habits, is set loose among the iron pots of this mechanistic orientation, the clay vessel of Jewish archaism suffers that fortune which is due and coming to clay vessels among the iron pots. His beautifully rounded heirloom, trade-marked "B.C.," goes to pieces between his hands, and they are left empty. He is divested of those archaic conventional preconceptions which will not comport with the intellectual environment in which he finds himself. But he is not thereby invested with the gentile's peculiar heritage of conventional preconceptions which have stood over, by inertia of habit, out of the gentile past, which go, on the one hand, to make the safe and sane gentile, conservative and complacent, and which conduce also, on the other hand, to blur the safe and sane gentile's intellectual vision, and to leave him intellectually sessile.

The young Jew finds his own heritage of usage and outlook untenable; but this does not mean that he therefore will take over and inwardly assimilate the traditions of usage and outlook which the gentile world has to offer; or at the most he does not uncritically take over all the intellectual prepossessions that are always standing over among the substantial citizens of the republic of learning. The idols of his own tribe have crumbled in decay and no longer cumber the ground, but that release does not induce him to set up a new line of idols borrowed from an alien tribe to do the same disservice. By consequence he is in a peculiar degree exposed to the unmediated facts of the current situation; and in a peculiar degree, therefore, he takes his orientation from the run of the facts as he finds them, rather than from the traditional interpretation of analogous facts in the past. In short, he is a skeptic by force of circumstances over which he has no control. Which comes to saying that he is in line to become a guide and leader of men in that intellectual enterprise out of which comes the increase and diffusion of knowledge among men, provided always that he is by native gift endowed with that net modicum of intelligence which takes effect in the play of the idle curiosity.

Intellectually he is likely to become an alien; spiritually he is more than likely to remain a Jew; for the heartstrings of affection and consuetude are tied early, and they are not readily retied in after life. Nor does the animus with which the community of safe and sane gentiles is wont to meet him conduce at all to his personal incorporation in that community, whatever may befall the intellectual assets which he brings. Their people need not become his people nor their gods his gods, and indeed the provocation is forever and irritably present all over the place to turn back from following after them. The most amiable share in the gentile community's life that is likely to fall to his lot is that of being interned. One who goes away from home will come to see many unfamiliar things, and to take note of them; but it does not follow that he will swear by all the strange gods whom he meets along the road.

As bearing on the Zionist's enterprise in isolation and nationality, this fable appears to teach a two-fold moral: If the adventure is carried to that consummate outcome which seems to be aimed at, it should apparently be due to be crowned with a large national complacency and, possibly, a profound and self-sufficient content on the part of the Chosen People domiciled once more in the Chosen Land; and when and in so far as the Jewish people in this way turn inward on themselves, their prospective contribution to the world's intellectual output should, in the light of the historical evidence, fairly be expected to take on the complexion of Talmudic lore, rather than that character of free-swung skeptical initiative which their renegades have habitually infused into the pursuit of the modern sciences abroad among the nations. Doubtless, even so the supply of Jewish renegades would not altogether cease, though it should presumably fall off to a relatively inconsiderable residue. And not all renegades are fit guides and leaders of men on the quest of knowledge, nor is their dominant incentive always or ordinarily the quest of the idle curiosity.

There should be some loss to Christendom at large, and there might be some gain to the repatriated Children of Israel. It is a sufficiently difficult choice between a life of complacent futility at home and a thankless quest of unprofitable knowledge abroad. It is, after all, a matter of the drift of circumstance; and behind that lies a question of taste, about which there is no disputing.